COVER CARS
Front, lower: 365 GT4/BB, owned by Bill Harrah/Modern Classic
                Motors
      upper: 365 GTB/4, owned by Ken Starbird
Back, lower: 250 GTO, owned by Steve Earle
      upper: 250 LM, owned by Steve Earle (photo by Steve Earle)

To Enzo Ferrari: His foresight, dedication,
and perseverance made all this possible.

FERRARI The Gran Turismo & Competition Berlinettas

CONTENTS

FOREWORD

Ferrari development—from the first 1500cc Type 125 in 1947 through the 250 GTO and 250/330 LMB of 1963—followed a pattern of improving a tried and proven design. The engine, whether four, six or 12 cylinders, was in front, driving the rear wheels.

The front suspension was independent from the start, but a change was made from a transverse leaf to coil springs in 1955.

The rear suspension on most models was a live axle with semi-elliptic springs and twin parallel trailing arms for axle location. De Dion axles with transverse leaf, and full independent with A-arms and coil springs were also tried.

In 1960 Ferrari built his first "rear engined" (more correctly a mid-engine as the powerplant was behind the driver but ahead of the rear axle) car for Formula 1. The following year he built a mid-engined sports/racing car.

Ferrari's competitors, some spectators, and most journalists, thought Ferrari to be slow to adopt a "modern" design. Cooper had been competing successfully with mid-engined GP cars since the start of the 1959 season, Lotus introduced the mid-engined car in 1960 and

Porsche had built rear- or mid-engined cars since the company started producing cars in 1947.

Ferrari was slow to change the basic concept of his cars and while many reasons or excuses can be offered, I think he simply didn't want to tamper with a winning combination until he had to. And history, most often, backs his philosophy.

Temporary set-backs at the hands of Mercedes-Benz, Jaguar, Maserati, Aston Martin, Porsche or Cobra plagued Ferrari but none could put a perminent crimp in Ferrari fortunes.

Ferrari's front-engined, rear-drive "conventional" sports and GT cars (particularly the 250 GT berlinettas and Testa Rossas) won a tremendous number of races both as factory and private entries.

It is significant that Ferrari's cars continued to be winners during and after the switch to mid-engine, all-independent chassis, and then later going back to front-mounted engines with independent rear suspensions.

No matter what configuration Ferrari chose, it seemed to be at least somewhat, if not totally, successful. The secret, if you can call it that, being that he seldom built an *all* new car. A new engine, a new gearbox, a new rear suspension or even a different engine location, but never all of them at once (a lesson other race car builders could profit from).

And while Mercedes-Benz, Aston Martin, Jaguar and Maserati were in and out of competition, Ferrari was always active—and almost always in Grand Prix, Sports/GT, and Prototype classes at the same time.

The result is not only a tremendous number of racing and touring victories, but 20 World Manufacturers Championships (as of 1976), all of which have contributed to the Ferrari mystique—a mystique and enthusiasm enjoyed by few car manufacturers.

There is a difference of opinion about which period of Ferrari's short history as a car builder (less than 30 years as this is written) is most interesting. The first decade, from 1947 through 1957, has to be considered, because "multi" cylinder engines had been tried many times in racing and with the exception of Mercedes-Benz and Auto Union in the late Thirties, met with little success until Ferrari brought out a V-12 in 1947.

My vote, however, goes to the second and third decade because even though the marque was in its real, and exciting, development period during the first 10 years, so few Ferraris were made (less than 1000) that they could only be vicariously enjoyed by most enthusiasts—watching them race, reading about them in magazines, and, rarely, seeing one up close at a *Concours d'Elegance* or auto show.

But from the early Sixties the enthusiasm, the economy, and the availability came together at the right time in a combination that allowed the greatest actual involvement by Ferrari enthusiasts. New Ferraris were costly—about $12,500 at the time—but enough had been sold around the world that used ones in all conditions between superb and basket cases were available.

The result was a tremendous increase in enthusiasm and participation in the mistique by enthusiasts. Unfortunately, for those who have not yet owned a Ferrari, a later result was the unexpected increase in the value of these cars.

Those who have been able to own one of these exciting vehicles are among a fortunate few who are legitimately envied by their less adventuresome (and less fortunate) peers.

Dean Batchelor

August 24, 1963, and Graham Hill shows why he was World Champion in 1962 by winning the Tourist Trophy at Goodwood, England in a right hand drive GTO, No.

4399. Mike Parkes was 2nd in another GTO, Roy Salvadori was 3rd in an Aston Martin and Jack Sears was 4th in an E-Type Jaguar.

250 GTO

The first Ferrari berlinetta was an open 166 S re-bodied with closed bodywork which, driven by Clemente Biondetti, won the 1948 Mille Miglia. That victory was Ferrari's first in the 1000 mile race around Italy, the first for a closed Ferrari, and the race gave its name to Ferrari models that would continue from the 166 through 212, 250, 340, and 375—into 1954.

Ferrari continued to build closed cars for both grand touring and competition, and the factory's main efforts were directed toward all-out competition on one hand—Formula 1 and 2 Grand Prix, and sports racing—and roadable GT cars on the other.

In 1955, however, Pierre Levegh's tragic accident at Le Mans caused the FIA (Federation Internationale de l'Automobile) to write rules for the upcoming season that would hopefully bring "sports" car racing back to the original intent, i.e. genuine dual-purpose automobiles.

Mercedes-Benz had the 300 SL, Aston Martin the DB-2, Jaguar the XK series, and Ferrari the 250 GT in various forms. Ferrari, with help from Pininfarina (and soon, Scaglietti), developed a designed-for-competition berlinetta in late 1955.

This fastback, lightweight coupe was on the standard 250 GT 2600mm (102.3-inch) wheelbase and was, as required by FIA regs, a dual-purpose car. The new 250 GT berlinettas virtually dominated GT racing classes wherever they raced in 1956, 1957 and 1958, and after three straight victories in the Tour de France, the model was nicknamed the TDF.

In 1959, the 250 GT underwent its first major redesign with a shorter wheelbase (2400mm, or 94.5 inches) and a new body designed by Pininfarina and once again built by Scaglietti. The chassis modifications were handled by Giotto Bizzarrini, who had engineered

The cockpit of the ex-Jean Guichet 1963 Tour de France winning GTO No. 5111.

This lightweight 250 berlinetta, with Pininfarina bodywork that was similar to his 400 Superamerica, was entered at Le Mans in 1961 for Fernand Tavano and Giancarlo Baghetti. Stirling Moss later drove it in the Daytona 3-hour race February 11, 1962.

the previous longer wheelbase car as well.

The new model, referred to as swb (for short wheelbase) continued the winning ways of the lwb coupes and became the car to beat in the GT classes—from races to rallies. The lighter weight and increased horsepower (up to 280) made the car faster in both acceleration and top speed, the shorter wheelbase gave it better manuverability, and it was victorious in both the hands of factory drivers and private entrants. The short wheelbase models were built through 1962 and served as the basis for a newer, lighter, faster and more competitive berlinetta to come.

At the 24 Hours of Le Mans, in June 1961, a lightweight berlinetta on the 2400mm chassis but carrying Pininfarina bodywork derived from his 1961 Superfast II (on a 410 Superamerica chassis), was entered for Fernand Tavano and Giancarlo Baghetti.

The engine was similar to the 250 Testa Rossa which, with its six

38 DCN Webers, put out 300 bhp at 7500 rpm. The car was placed as high as 7th overall, but dropped out in the 13th hour with engine problems. Stirling Moss later drove it to 4th overall in the Daytona 3-hour race February 11, 1962.

The new GTO (for Grand Touring Omologato) was a striking design—lower and sleeker than previous berlinettas, and its aluminum bodywork reflected the results of aerodynamic experiments carried out by Ferrari after the 1961 Le Mans car had suffered from front end lift at speed.

The experimental "mule" was a 250 swb referred to as the "anteater", which was driven by Ferrari test drivers to check the results of running changes being made in the body shape. The nose was longer and lower than that used on the prototype, two vertical slots were cut into the front fender sides just ahead of the doors to let out under-hood air, and the tail was higher and squared-off compared to either the previous long or short wheelbase GTs. It had three Weber 46 DCZ carburetors and a 4-speed gearbox.

The new GTO, as shown to the press in February 1962 displayed all the results of the interim testing and the handsome coupe designed by the Ferrari engineering team and built by Scaglietti ended at the rear with a full Kamm-type tail. The Kamm theory, somewhat over-simplified, was that if the departure angle (slope) of the roof was slight, then it is better to chop the tail off square rather than to extend it for better airflow—thus reducing both overhang and weight without materially affecting aerodynamics.

The GTO shown to the press was in the expected Ferrari red, but carried nose-to-tail striping in the Italian tri-colors (red, white and green), and had no spoiler at the rear. A spoiler was tacked on when the car made its competition debut at Sebring in March, where it finished 2nd overall and 1st in GT class, driven by Phil Hill and Olivier Gendebien. Subsequent GTOs also had spoilers added to the existing bodywork, but later GTOs had the spoiler built in as part of the actual Scaglietti bodywork.

Ferrari's experimental "mule" was driven by Willy Mairesse (far right) to check the results of running changes being made in the body shape. The chassis was a 250 swb and the final result was the 250 GTO shown to the press (next page) in February 1962.

The cleanest GTO built was the first, No 3223, shown to the press in February 1962. It had no spoiler on the rear, and the Ferrari-red paint was accented by the nose-to-tail red, white and green Italian tri-colors with a thin white outline stripe. A tacked-on spoiler was added at Sebring and later this feature became part of the Scaglietti bodywork.

The GTO engine is a magnificent work of art as well as one of the most reliable racing powerplants ever built. It was equally at home on the track at Le Mans, in the Tour de France or motoring up U.S. 395. The GTO driver traveled light as once the spare wheel and tool kit went in there was little room for anything else.

The chassis of the GTO differed from the swb berlinetta in only minor respects, but these differences apparently were to help performance as much as did the sleeker body configuration.

Front suspension was still unequal length A-arms and concentric coil springs and tubular shock absorbers. At the rear, Ing. Bizzarrini wanted to use coil springs in place of semi-elliptics but felt that the car might not be homologated in the GT category if chassis changes were too radical, so he retained the live axle and semi-elliptics but added coils around the tubular shocks as "compensators." Longitudinal axle location, and torque reaction, was by two parallel trailing arms on each side. Lateral location was by a Watt link.

The frame was still made up of welded steel tubing with elliptical-section main members as before, but whereas the minor axis of the earlier swb frame tubing was about 70% of the major dimension, in the GTO the minor dimension was about 50% (as in late short wheelbase models) resulting in some weight saving without apparently weakening the structure.

The GTO engine was similar to the Testa Rossa and dry-sump lubrication was used on the GTO right from the beginning (the first TRs had wet-sumps, switching to a dry-sump system after the 1959 Le Mans 24-hour race).

Horsepower, as on the TR and 1961 racing berlinettas, was rated at 300 at 7500 rpm with the red-line at 8500 rpm. Six 38 DCN twin-choke Webers were used and the exhaust headers were divided into groups of three equal-length pipes which then converged into a single pipe to the rear on each side—also like the 1961 swb competition models.

Drive from the engine was taken through a single dry-plate clutch into a 5-speed transmission with all five speeds synchronized. Four-wheel disc brakes were used, as on the swb berlinetta. The GTO was 6.6 inches longer and 3.5 inches lower than the short wheelbase berlinetta.

On May 6, 1962, Scarlatti and Ferraro drove a GTO to 4th overall and 1st in GT class in the Targa Florio. The following week, at

Silverstone, England, Mike Parkes and Masten Gregory were 1st and 2nd in 250 GTOs—ahead of Graham Hill in an E-Type Jaguar and Jim Clark in an Aston Martin DB4/GT Zagato.

For the Nurburgring 1000-km race on May 27, Ferrari entered a prototype GTO with a 400 Superamerica 4-liter engine. Ferrari favored the change to GT cars (which had a 3 liter limit in 1962) for the Manufacturer's Championship but couldn't resist the challenge of the new 4 liter prototype class.

The engine of this 4 liter "GTO", No. 3765, was initially pretty much a 400 SA engine with dry sump. Three Weber 46 DCF3 carburetors were used, but 38 DCN Webers were later added for Le Mans.

Mike Parkes and Willy Mairesse drove the 4-liter GTO to 2nd overall. The 3-liter GTO of Umberto Maglioli and Gottfried Kochert was leading the GT class but was eliminated when the starter failed after a pit stop. Giorgio Scarlatti crashed his 250 GTO on the sixth lap of this difficult Nurburgring circuit and a 1960 swb berlinetta driven by Nocker/Seidel won the GT class.

The new 250 GTOs finished 1st and 3rd at Mallory Park, England, on June 11, 1962, driven by Mike Parkes and John Surtees, with Graham Hill's E-Type Jaguar sandwiched between in 2nd place.

Two weeks later, at the Le Mans 24-hour event, a 250 GTO was 1st in class and 2nd overall (Pierre Noblet/Jean Guichet) behind the Hill/Gendebien 4-liter Ferrari spyder. GTOs were also 3rd (Leon "Elde"

Mike Parkes and Willy Mairesse drove the 4-liter GTO Prototype, to 2nd place in the Nurburgring 1000km race on May 27, 1962. The engine was a 400 SA with dry-sump lubrication and three 38 DCN Webers. The car carried race number 120 at Nurburgring. A similar car, with race number 7 was run at Le Mans where it was driven by Parkes and Lorenzo Bandini. Parkes put the car, No. 3765, in the sand at Mulsanne while leading the first lap and it later expired from sand damage.

Dernier/Jean Beurlys), 6th (Bob Grossman/Fireball Roberts) and Ed Hugus and George Reed were 9th in the prototype Farina-bodied GTO that had been driven at Le Mans the year before by Tavano and Baghetti. The 4-liter GTO started fast with Parkes at the wheel, but ended up in the sand bank at Mulsanne and by the time Parkes dug it out and turned it over to co-driver Bandini, it was overheating from sand damage to the radiator and the car was retired in the seventh hour.

A peculiar-looking pseudo GTO, nicknamed "breadvan," made its initial competition appearance at Le Mans and, driven by Carlo Abate/Colin Davis, ran as high as 7th overall before dropping out with transmission problems.

The BRSCC races at Brands Hatch, England, on August 6, 1962,

The Tommy Hitchcock/Prince Tchokotoua GTO (No. 3647) was 8th overall and 5th in
GT class in the 1963 Targa Florio.

were a Ferrari benefit with Mike Parkes finishing 1st in the Peco Trophy Race in a 250 GTO, ahead of five other GTOs, and Graham Hill's E-Type Jag. A few hours later Parkes won the Guards Trophy Race with a Ferrari 246 spyder. The breadvan finished 4th in this race, driven by Abate.

Another Ferrari triumph occured at the Tourist Trophy Races at Goodwood, England, on August 18th. Six Ferrari berlinettas were entered against three Zagato-bodied Aston Martin DB4/GTs, and three E-Type Jaguars. A right hand drive GTO, driven by Innes Ireland was 1st, followed by the GTOs of Graham Hill and Mike Parkes, Roy Salvadori in a Jaguar, then David Piper's GTO.

In September, 1962, Ferrari won the Tour de France for the marque's 7th straight victory in that event, but it was a swb berlinetta driven by Simon/Dupeyron that won—beating the GTOs of Schlesser/Orieller, Darvil/Langlois, Piper/Marguelis, Bianchi/Dubois and the 1961 swb of De Lageneste/Berglin.

The 1000-km of Paris, held at Montlhery on October 21, finished the 1962 European season and Ferraris were 1st (Ricardo and Pedro Rodriguez, 250 GTO), 2nd (Surtees/Parkes, 250 GTO), 3rd (Davis/Scarfiotti, breadvan), 4th (Guichet/Noblet, 250 GTO), 5th (Mairesse/Bianchi, 250 GTO), and 6th (Simon/Berger, 1961 250 swb).

This was the last race that the Rodriguez brothers would co-drive for Ferrari, as Ricardo was killed in a crash during practice for the 1962 Mexican Grand Prix.

Ferrari's annual press conference—for 1963—was held on December 1, 1962, even though his 1963 cars were not ready to be shown. Ferrari said that few, if any, more GTOs would be built because in his opinion they were too fast for all but a handful of top drivers. At the end of 1962, 25 GTOs had been built including two 4-liter coupes, and 10 more GTOs (including one 4-liter) would be built in 1963.

The GTO was reaffirmed as a Group III Gran Turismo by the CSI (Commission Sportive Internationale) of the FIA.

Ferrari's serial numbering system normally gave even numbers to competition cars and odd numbers to the more normal touring cars, but all GTOs carried odd numbers—further emphasizing Ferrari's desire to consider the GTO a genuine dual-purpose car.

The 1963 series of GT races started off well for Ferrari when Pedro Rodriguez won the 3-hour Daytona Continental on February 17, in a GTO owned by Mamie Spears Reynolds. Roger Penske was 2nd in John Mecom's GTO.

At Sebring, on March 23, the new Ferrari 250 Ps were 1st and 2nd; the 3rd place car was the 4-liter prototype 1962 Le Mans winner. GTOs were 4th (Roger Penske/Augie Pabst), 5th (Carlo Abate/Juan Bordeu), 6th (Richie Ginther/Innes Ireland), 13th (Jo Bonnier/John Cannon), 14th (David Piper/Bill Cantrell) and 18th (Charlie Hayes/Doug Thiem/Bob Grossman).

Bulgari and Grana were 1st in GT and 4th overall at the Targa Florio, Juan Bordeu/Giorgio Scarlatti were 6th, Tommy Hitchcock/Prince Tchokotoua were 8th and Nicolosi/Taramazzo were 13th, all in 250 GTOs.

Competition for the GTO in GT racing had been almost lacking from its debut at Sebring in 1962 until the Nurburgring 1000-km race on May 19, 1963. There a lightweight, aluminum-bodied Jaguar E-Type roadster, driven by Peter Lindner led the 1st lap, and was 3rd overall for many laps, but the car expired with a blown engine on the 23rd of 44 laps.

The Noblet/Guichet 250 GTO was 2nd overall behind the Surtees/Mairesse 250 P, while the Abate/Maglioli TRI/61 was 3rd, Elde/Van Ophem were 5th in a Bizzarrini-Drogo pseudo GTO, Piper/Cantrell and Lohstratter/Felder were 6th and 7th in production 250 GTOs, and Kerrison/Salmon were 8th in another Bizzarrini-Drogo special "GTO."

At Le Mans, on June 15–16, 1963, the Beurlys/Langlois 250 GTO was 2nd overall at 112.5 mph (the winning Scarfiotti/Bandini 250 P averaged 118.5 mph) and the Elde/Dumay GTO was 4th. Abate crashed the GTO he shared with Tavano. This was the fastest GTO entered, recording 174 mph on the Mulsanne straight during the race.

GTOs were 1st (Graham Hill), 2nd (Mike Parkes), 5th (David Piper) and 8th (Roger Penske) in the Tourist Trophy at Goodwood, England, on August 24, giving Ferrari his fourth straight TT victory. The Chris Kerrison Bizzarrini-Drogo special was 10th, despite many pit stops for ignition malfunctions.

Mike Parkes' GTO was 2nd overall and 1st in the 3-liter GT class at the Coppa Inter-Europa on September 8th. Two weeks later, the GTOs of Jean Guichet/Jose Behra and Mauro Bianchi/Carlo Abate were 1st and 2nd in the Tour de France giving Ferrari his eighth straight Tour win.

The last event of 1963 was at Nassau, where Mike Gammino drove his GTO to 1st in GT and 2nd overall in the Nassau Tourist Trophy Race.

Graham Hill's right hand drive GTO was 2nd to Innes Ireland's similar car (by 3.4 seconds) at the 1962 Tourist Trophy race at Goodwood, England.

In 1963 Ferrari had experienced his first real competition for the GTO in the form of the lightweight E-Type Jaguars. In 1964, the second wave hit the shore in the form of English AC Aces with American Ford V-8 engines—more commonly known as Cobras. These lightweight roadsters, with powerful and reliable Ford ohv engines, created by Carroll Shelby, were potent machines and strong competitors.

Ferrari had requested homologation of his new 250 LM from the CSI, but was turned down on the basis that not enough cars had been built to satisfy the required 100 units. This was true, of course, but

the GTO had been homologated even before the first model had competed in its first race at Sebring—the reason being that it was a "logical extension of the previous 250 (2993cc V-12s) series of Gran Turismo cars." So what worked for Ferrari on the GTO, did not work for him on the LM.

Nurburgring 1000km race, 1964. The Mike Parkes/Jean Guichet (left) series II GTO, No. 5573, finished 2nd overall, behind the Scarfiotti/Vaccarella 275 P, and 1st in class. Freiburg Hillclimb, 1964—Lodovico Scarfiotti's Series II GTO was 1st in class, 4th overall.

The 1964 version of the GTO shared the same chassis but was visually different from the '62-'63 cars, yet it was as strikingly handsome as the first version in its own way. A wide air inlet at the front replaced the small elliptical opening with its supplemental air inlets. An almost wrap-around, sharply raked windshield in a short cab, set well back on the Scaglietti-built body, with buttress-type sail panels and inset rear window gave the series II GTO a rakish look that set it totally apart from the norm (this configuration was the inspiration for the 1968 Corvette Stingray). The 1964 GTO was 4.3 inches shorter, 2.3 inches wider and 2.1 inches lower than the series I models.

The 1964 series II GTO demonstrated early that its beauty wasn't just skin deep when the first of the new series won the 2000-km of Daytona (Phil Hill/Pedro Rodriguez) fresh off the boat from Italy. The Piper/Bianchi GTO was 2nd and the Hansgen/Grossman GTO was 3rd. A Cobra was 4th, a GTO 5th, Cobras 7th and 10th and another GTO 11th. All these GTOs except the 1st place car were series I fastback berlinettas.

At Sebring, on March 21, 1964, the best finish by a GTO was 7th overall and 1st in 2000-3000cc GT class, driven by Piper/Rodriguez/Gammino.

Graham Hill eaked out a narrow victory (0.8 seconds) in a GTO 64 at Goodwood, England, on Easter Monday, over Jack Sears' Cobra. David Piper was 3rd in another GTO.

At the Targa Florio, on April 26, 1964, the GTO 64 of Ferlaino/Taramazzo was 5th overall—behind two Porsche 904 GTs and two Alfa Romeo GTZs, winning the GT III category to collect points for Ferrari toward the Manufacturer's Championship. The first Cobra was the Dan Gurney/Jerry Grant car in 8th place. The Guichet/Facetti GTO 64 retired while leading and the Fortinbras/"Ulisse" GTO dropped out in the sixth lap of the 10 lap race. Series I GTOs finished 9th (Norinder/Truberg), 10th (Bourillot/de Bourbon Y Parma) and 12th (Nicolosi/Zanardelli).

Series II GTOs, while generally attractive, had their bad angles—and this one, the Beurlys/Bianchi car at Le Mans in 1964, is made grotesque by the camera's long lens.

This view of a Series II GTO illustrates why it's often thought of as a race car with a top, and how it inspired the 1968 Corvette body shape.

At Silverstone, England, on May 2, Graham Hill won the GT race in a GTO 64, and two weeks later at the Spa-Francorchamps 500-km race Mike Parkes, Jean Guichet and Lorenzo Bandini were 1st, 2nd and 3rd in GTO 64s (Parkes' was right-hand-drive) and David Piper was 4th in his 1963 GTO.

The Ford GT made its competition debut at the Nurburgring 1000-km race on May 31, 1964 and, driven by Phil Hill, posted second fastest qualifying time but did not finish the race because of rear suspension failure on the 16th lap. The race was won by Lodovico Scarfiotti and Nino Vaccarella in a Ferrari 275 P and the Parkes/Guichet GTO 64 was 2nd overall and 1st in GT class. Another GTO 64 driven by Bianchi/Van Ophem was 4th overall. Mechanical failures and bad luck ganged up on the Shelby Cobras and the best placed Cobra was 23rd with the highest finishing E-Type Jaguar 25th.

The Le Mans 24-hour race on June 20–21 was a different story.

Ferrari spyders finished 1-2-3 but a Cobra Daytona coupe driven by Dan Gurney and Bob Bondurant was 4th overall and 1st in the GT category. The Beurlys/Bianchi GTO 64 was 5th overall and 2nd in GT with a 115.8 mph race average in spite of losing one lap to replace the brake pads.

Ferrari swept the Reims 12-hour race on July 5th with 250 Ps 1st and 2nd, and GTO 64s 3rd (Parkes/Scarfiotti) and 4th (Piper/Maggs).

Bob Bondurant brought bad news for Ferrari by winning the Freiburg hill climb August 9th in a team Cobra, ahead of Scarfiotti's GTO 64. Three weeks later, in the Tourist Trophy at Goodwood, a Ferrari 330 P spyder was 1st and 250 LM 2nd, but Cobras were 3rd, 4th and 5th, beating out the Innes Ireland GTO 64 which was 6th, and the GTO 64s of Ginther and Maggs which were 9th and 10th. John Surtees was hospitalized after crashing the NART GTO 64.

The Tour de France, always an important event because of its

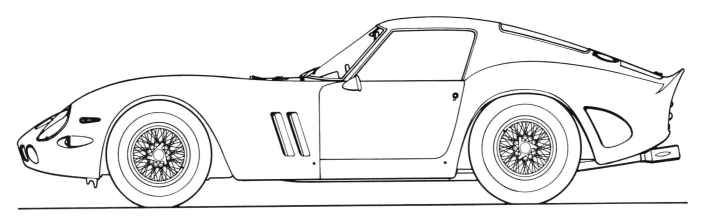

250 GTO

1/24 scale drawing based on Ferrari No. 4293

ENGINE

Type ....Colombo-based, water-cooled, 60 degree V-12
Bore/stroke, mm/inches 73.0/58.8, 2.875/2.315
Displacement, cc/cubic inches 2953/180.0
Valve operation: Single overhead camshaft on each bank with roller followers and rocker arms to inclined valves
Valve springs ....Coil
Camshaft drive...Chain
Ignition ....Two Marelli distributors
Sparkplugs/cyl ....One
Compression ratio 9.8:1
Carburetion ....Six Weber 38 DCN twin-choke, downdraft
BHP (Mfg.) ....295 @ 7400 rpm

DRIVE TRAIN

Clutch ....Single dry-plate
Transmission: Five-speed, 2–5 synchronized, direct drive in 5th gear
Rear axle..Live
Axle ratios 3.67, 3.78, 4.00, 4.25, 4.55, 4.57, 4.86:1

CHASSIS

Frame ....Welded tubular steel
Wheelbase, mm/inches 2400/94.5
Track, front, mm/inches 1354/53.3
    rear, mm/inches.....................................1350/53.1
Front suspension: Independent, unequal-length A-arms, coil springs
Rear suspension: Live axle, semi-elliptic springs and parallel trailing arms on each side
Shock absorbers...Tubular
Brakes ....Disc
Tire size, front/rear...............................5.50/7.00 x 15
Wheels................................Borrani wire, center-lock, knock-off

GENERAL

Length overall, mm/inches 4400/173.2
Width 1675/65.9
Height..1245/49.0
Body builder ....Scaglietti

influence on the car-buying public (the Tour is essentially a high speed rally and shows cars in the context that the public would be more likely to identify with than they could ever hope to do in racing) was even more important in 1964 because it counted toward the Manufacturer's Championship for the first time.

The 1964 Tour covered 3800 miles in France and northern Italy with checkpoints along the way. Eight races were scheduled, at Reims, Rouen, Le Mans, Cognac, Pau, Albi, Clermont-Ferrand, and Monza. Eight hill climbs were also included.

At the Lille start, 120 cars departed, and 38 survived to the finish at Nice. Anne Soisbault and Nicole Roare won the Coupes des Dames in a GTO 64, placing 9th in the Tour. Overall Tour winners were Bianchi and Berger, with Guichet and de Bourbon Y Parma 2nd—both cars were 1962-63 style GTOs—giving Ferrari his 9th straight Tour de France victory. This also gave Ferrari the 1964 Manufacturer's Championship with 84.6 points to 78.3 for Shelby's Cobras.

Ferrari entered the 1000-km of Paris, at Montlhery, on October 11, against strong opposition from Porsche and Jaguar. Jo Schlesser and Pedro Rodriguez finished 2nd in a GTO 64 behind the Ferrari 330 P of Hill/Bonnier. Piper and Maggs were 4th and Bianchi/Van Ophem were 5th in Series I GTOs.

Ferrari was frustrated because he could not get the 250 LM homologated as a GT car, but it had made the 250 GTO obsolete, so he announced at his December press conference that he would not contest the GT category in 1965.

GTOs continued to be raced successfully by private entrants and Ravetto and Starabba won the GT class at the Targa Florio in 1965 with a GTO 64.

The GTO was supposedly the last front-engined competition car built by Ferrari, although later, special versions of the 275 GTB and 365 GTB/4 would be raced successfully even though originally designed primarily for normal road use.

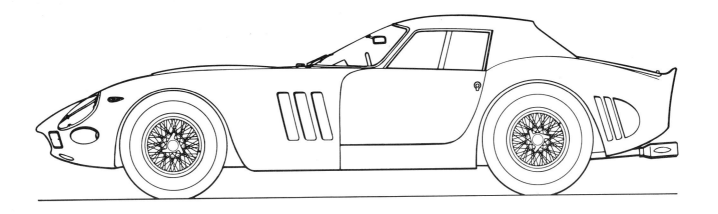

1/24 scale drawing based on Ferrari No. 5575

ENGINE

Type .... Colombo-based, water-cooled, 60 degree V-12
Bore/stroke, mm/inches 73.0/58.8, 2.875/2.315
Displacement, cc/cubic inches 2953/180.0
Valve operation: Single overhead camshaft on each bank with roller followers and rocker arms to inclined valves
Valve springs .... Coil
Camshaft drive .... Chain
Ignition .... Two Marelli distributors
Sparkplugs/cyl .... One
Compression ratio 9.8:1
Carburetion .... Six Weber 38 DCN twin-choke, downdraft
BHP (Mfg.) .... 300 @ 7700 rpm

DRIVE TRAIN

Clutch .... Single dry-plate
Transmission: Five-speed, 2-5 synchronized, direct drive in 5th gear
Rear axle .... Live
Axle ratios 3.67, 3.78, 4.00, 4.25, 4.55, 4.57, 4.86:1

CHASSIS

Frame .... Welded tubular steel
Wheelbase, mm/inches 2400/94.5
Track, front, mm/inches 1377/54.2
      rear, mm/inches 1426/56.1
Front suspension: Independent, unequal-length A-arms, coil springs
Rear suspension: Live axle, semi-elliptic springs and parallel trailing arms on each side
Shock absorbers .... Tubular
Brakes .... Disc
Tire size, front/rear .... 5.50/7.00 x 15
Wheels .... Borrani wire, center-lock, knock-off

GENERAL

Length overall, mm/inches 4210/165.7
Width 1760/69.3
Height 1140/44.9
Body builder .... Scaglietti

Pseudo GTO

The pseudo GTOs were built in 1962—all on 250 GT short wheelbase chassis—by the late Piero Drogo's Modena Sports Cars. The mechanical work was by Giorgio Neri and Luciano Bonacini with technical assistance from Giotto Bizzarrini, who had been responsible for the chassis development of the swb Ferrari 250 GTs as well as the 250 GTOs.

The most famous of the three fake GTOs was the "breadvan" built for Count Volpi's Scuderia Republica de Venezia. This car (No. 2819) had started life as an aluminum-bodied swb berlinetta purchased by Olivier Gendebien on Sept. 11, 1961, for himself and Lucien Bianchi to drive in the Tour de France, where they finished 2nd behind Mairesse/Berger in another swb 250.

The breadvan vaguely resembled a GTO from the cockpit forward, but from there back, it was unique unto itself. The top went almost straight back to the Kamm-type, truncated tail, which housed the rear window, complete with wiper, set into an opening hatch.

In this form, it was entered in four races in 1962; Le Mans, the Guards Trophy and Peco Trophy (both at Brands Hatch, England), and the 1000km of Montlhery where it finished 3rd (Davis/Scarfiotti) for its best final placing.

The second imitation GTO to appear resembled the real thing only in the windshield and side window area and even there was not identical. This car, a right hand drive 250 swb No. 2735 GT, had been sold to Rob Walker on May 30, 1961. Driven by Stirling Moss, the car had one dnf (Le Mans), one dns (Tour de France) and five 1st place finishes: Brands Hatch Bank Holiday, Brands Hatch Peco Trophy, Goodwood TT, British Empire Trophy at Silverstone, and the Nassau TT in December—all in 1961.

The "breadvan," in Serenissima colors, at start of Ollon-Villars Hillclimb.

The "breadvan," right, goes through the esses at Le Mans in 1962. Below, the Chris Kerrison rebodied swb No. 2735, at Nurburgring where it finished 10th overall, co-driven by Mike Salmon.

In its re-bodied, imitation GTO form, Chris Kerrison campaigned the car into 1964 with a 1st at the Portugal GP, 6th at Zolder, Belgium, and 10th at the Nurburgring being his best finishes.

The third "counterfeit" GTO, chassis No. 2053, was sold to C. Toselli on Aug. 2, 1960. At that time it also was a normal 250 GT swb berlinetta, and Toselli achieved a 1st, 3rd and 6th at minor events in 1960. The car was subsequently purchased by Scuderia Francorchamps and crashed at Le Mans in 1962.

Equipe National Belge then bought the car and had it rebuilt by Drogo into one of the ugliest of all competition Ferrari berlinettas, with a twin-nostril nose of absurd design. In this form it managed a 4th at Spa-Francorchamps and a 5th overall at Nurburgring.

In 1963, the E.N.B. car was raced by M. Remordu, who gained four 1st places and one 6th place in non-championship events. A crash at Spa destroyed the car in 1964.

The three re-bodied, re-engineered GT berlinettas retained the basic chassis of the swb berlinetta but incorporated certain GTO features such as the concentric "helper" coil springs around the rear tubular koni shocks—as used by Bizzarrini on the factory GTOs.

All three hybrids were lower than a genuine GTO although it is doubtful if the height of the cg was changed much. In all cases the cars turned out uglier and less successful than the cars they were hoping to beat. In the first two examples, the original swb GT was more successful than its successor, probably due to the owner/driver combination.

The Drogo rebodied swb No. 2053, carrying race number 59, was 5th overall at the Nurburgring 1000km in 1963. The rear view bears some similarity to a standard GTO.

250 LM

In November, 1962, a new mid-engined Ferrari V-12—the 250 P—made its debut at Monza and John Surtees, who had just joined Ferrari, broke the lap record with the car. Its engine was a virtually standard 3-liter Testa Rossa with six 38 DCN Webers and dry-sump lubrication. The chassis was one that was used for the Dino V-6 and V-8 mid-engined competition cars but with the wheelbase lengthened from 91.4 to 94.5 inches to accommodate the longer engine.

In November, 1963, a closed version of the 250 P called the LM (for Le Mans) was shown at the Paris auto show. Like the 250 P, the LM had 4-wheel independent suspension with fabricated tubular A-arms, coil springs, tubular shock absorbers and 4-wheel disc brakes (inboard at the rear).

The engine, based on the Testa Rossa, had the multiple-disc clutch mounted on the flywheel, between the engine and the transaxle (early 250 Ps were so equipped, but later versions had the clutch "outboard" behind the transaxle assembly). The un-synchronized 5-speed transmission had all indirect gears and allowed the dry-sump engine to be installed low in the chassis, thus lowering both the center of gravity and the frontal area.

The water radiator, an oil radiator, and the oil reservoir tank for the dry-sump lubrication system were mounted in the nose of the car.

The berlinetta bodywork was Pininfarina-designed and used a windshield and side windows that later appeared on the series II GTO. In fact, the entire top was similar on both cars with the vertical back window recessed between the buttress sail panels.

The first 250 LM had a completely undistinguished racing record. After the European auto shows were over, the car was sent to the U.S. where it was campaigned by NART (Luigi Chinetti's North

The 250 LM, dressed or undressed, shows its functional design and construction. After the first car, all 250 LMs had 275 engines but retained the 250 designation as Ferrari was seeking FIA homologation. Opposite page—one fastback 250 LM was made by extending rear window from roof to tail but was abandoned after Le Mans practice because of poor rear visibility. The Jochen Rindt (shown driving)/Masten Gregory 250 LM won Le Mans in 1965.

American Racing Team). At Daytona, in February, driven by Pedro Rodriguez, it retired with a broken fuel line. Buck Fulp drove it at the Augusta, Georgia, SCCA Nationals and it finished 8th. The car was then entered at Sebring for Tom O'Brien and Charlie Kolb and lasted only a short time before it caught fire and was totally destroyed.

The next appearance of a 250 LM was at the Le Mans trials in April 1964 (also appearing at the trials was a fastback LM which was never raced in that configuration because of poor rear vision). The LM was now equipped with a 275 engine as the original 73mm bore was increased to 77mm, resulting in a displacement of 3287.50cc. The engine was still equipped with six 38 DCN twin-choke Webers, but the compression ratio had been raised to 9.7:1 and the engine was rated at 330 bhp at 7700 rpm.

All subsequent 250 LMs had 275 engines (we can account for only one 250 LM with a 3-liter engine) but Ferrari didn't change the car's 250 designation as he didn't want to jeopardize the homologation proceedings. Many journalists and Ferrari enthusiasts have referred to these cars as 275 LMs, but Ferrari doesn't recognize this designation, so the cars will be referred to as 250 LMs in this book. As things turned out, Ferrari might as well have called them 275s as it took two years to get homologation papers from the FIA.

The racing record of the 250 LM didn't immediately improve even with more displacement and horsepower. Two were entered at the Nurburgring 1000-km race on May 31, 1964, for Umberto Maglioli/ Jochen Rindt and Jean Beurlys/Pierre Dumay. Neither car finished; the former crashed and the latter went out with suspension failure.

No 250 LMs were entered at Le Mans in June, and the first major victory for the car was at the 12-Hours of Reims on July 5. Jo Bonnier and Graham Hill drove a 3.3 liter 250 LM to 1st place at an average speed of 126 mph even though they had lost the use of 1st and 2nd gears. John Surtees and Lorenzo Bandini were 2nd in a similar car, in spite of losing time from a blown front tire during the race.

David Piper gained 2nd place in a 250 LM at the Tourist Trophy at Goodwood, England, on August 29 behind a new Ferrari 4-liter prototype.

Two victories in one day for the 250 LM were achieved when Walt Hansgen won the Road America 500 at Elkhart Lake in John Mecom's car, while at Mont Tremblant, Quebec, Pedro Rodriguez drove the NART 250 LM to 1st place.

On September 20, 1964, a 250 LM was 3rd at Bridgehampton, driven by Bob Grossman. The Elkhart Lake-winning 250 LM was driven by Augie Pabst, but failed to finish because of rear axle failure.

A 330 P (see chapter 5), driven by Pedro Rodriguez won the Canadian Grand Prix at Mosport, Ontario on September 26. Another 330 P was 2nd, driven by Lodovico Scarfiotti, Walt Hansgen was 4th in a 275 P and Bob Grossman finished 7th in a 250 LM.

The Ferrari 250 LM was considered a Gran Turismo car in Italy, and LMs were 1st (Nino Vaccarella), 2nd (Roy Salvadori) and 3rd (David Piper) at the Coppa Inter-Europa at Monza on September 6.

Far left, Paul Hawkins decelerates hard for a turn at Oulton Park, England. Left, the David Piper/Dick Attwood 250 LM was 4th in the Reims, France 12-hour race and below, car 232, Nicodemi/Lassona in the 1966 Targa Florio.

Right, the first 250 LM as shown at the factory in 1963 and, below, the David Piper 250 LM that was 7th overall at Le Mans in 1968, co-driven by Dick Attwood. Opposite page, recent photos of 250 LM No. 5061.

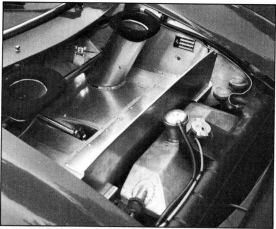

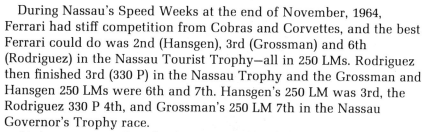

During Nassau's Speed Weeks at the end of November, 1964, Ferrari had stiff competition from Cobras and Corvettes, and the best Ferrari could do was 2nd (Hansgen), 3rd (Grossman) and 6th (Rodriguez) in the Nassau Tourist Trophy—all in 250 LMs. Rodriguez then finished 3rd (330 P) in the Nassau Trophy and the Grossman and Hansgen 250 LMs were 6th and 7th. Hansgen's 250 LM was 3rd, the Rodriguez 330 P 4th, and Grossman's 250 LM 7th in the Nassau Governor's Trophy race.

At the sports car Grand Prix of Angola, Italy, in December, 250 LMs were 1st and 2nd, driven by Willy Mairesse and Lucien Bianchi.

The 1964 season was good for Ferrari. GTO 64s won the Manufacturer's Championship; his mid-engined prototype spyders were unbeatable in their class, and 250 LM berlinettas won 10 major events, were 2nd in six and 3rd in four. Only 10 out of 35 250 LM entries failed to finish.

Ferrari did not campaign the 250 LM in 1965, but the cars were still being successfully raced by private entrants. Spencer Martin started the year off right by winning the Sandown Park, Australia, race February 21 in a 250 LM, and on March 21, Mairesse won at Zolder, Belgium, in a 250 LM.

At Sebring, on March 27, it was left up to private Ferrari entrants to represent the marque as Comm. Ferrari was feuding with the Sebring organizers over the inclusion of Appendix C sports cars with big American engines. The David Piper/Tony Maggs 250 LM finished

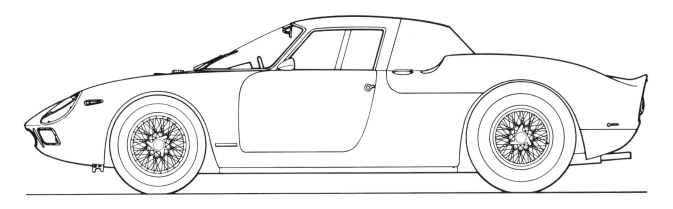

250 LM

1/24 scale drawing based on Ferrari No. 6107

ENGINE

Type ....Colombo-based, water-cooled, 60 degree V-12
Bore/stroke, mm/inches 77.0/58.8, 3.05/2.315
Displacement, cc/cubic inches......................3286/200.5
Valve operation: Single overhead camshaft on each bank with roller followers and rocker arms to inclined valves
Valve springs ....Coil
Camshaft drive...Chain
Ignition ....Two Marelli distributors
Sparkplugs/cyl ....One
Compression ratio 9.8:1
Carburetion ....Six Weber 38 DCN twin-choke, downdraft
BHP (Mfg.) ....305 @ 7500 rpm

DRIVE TRAIN

Clutch ....Single dry-plate
Transmission: Five-speed, non-synchromesh, direct drive in 5th gear
Rear axle ....Transaxle with halfshafts
Axle ratios 3.548, 4.038, 4.426, 4.842:1

CHASSIS

Frame ....Welded tubular steel
Wheelbase, mm/inches 2400/94.5
Track, front, mm/inches 1350/53.1
   rear, mm/inches..............................1340/52.8
Front suspension: Independent, unequal-length A-arms, coil springs
Rear suspension: Independent, unequal-length A-arms, coil springs
Shock absorbers....................................Tubular
Brakes ....Disc
Tire size, front/rear...........................5.50/7.00 x 15
Wheels................Borrani wire, center-lock, knock-off

GENERAL

Length overall, mm/inches 4270/168.1
Width 1700/66.9
Height..1115/43.9
Body builder ....Scaglietti (Pininfarina design)

Walt Hansgen won the 1964 Road America 500 at Elkhart Lake in John Mecom's 250 LM.

3rd behind the Chaparral and a Ford GT-40.

Fourteen Ferraris—mostly 275 P2 and 330 P2s—were entered in the 1000-km of Monza on April 25. Parkes and Jean Guichet were 1st in a 275 P2, John Surtees and Lodovico Scarfiotti were 2nd in a 330 P2 and 250 LMs were 6th (Innes Ireland/Mike Salmon) and 10th (Sighala/Luigi Taramazzo).

All the team Ferraris retired at the 24-Hour of Le Mans, June 19–20, but privately entered Ferraris finished 1st (Jochen Rindt/Masten Gregory—NART 250 LM), 2nd (Pierre Dumay/Gustaf Gosselin—Dumay's 250 LM), 3rd (Willy Mairesse/Jean Beurlys—275 GTB, also 1st in GT), 6th (Dieter Spoerry/Bohler—250 LM) and 7th.

Scuderia Ferrari did not enter the 12-Hours of Reims July 3–4, but there were many private entries. NART's 365 P2 (Rodriguez/Guichet) was 1st, Maranello Concessionaires' 365 P2 (Surtees/Parkes) was 2nd, Ecurie Francorchamps' 250 LM (Mairesse/Beurlys) was 3rd and David Piper's British Racing Green 250 LM (Piper/Dick Attwood) was 4th. Bob Bondurant and Jo Schlesser's Cobra was 5th, clinching the 1965 Manufacturer's Championship for Carroll Shelby.

The Enna Cup Race in Sicily, held on August 15, saw Ferrari 250 LMs finish 1st and 2nd (Mario Casoni and David Piper) with Cobra Daytona coupes 3rd and 4th (Bob Bondurant and Jack Sears).

The following week Jochen Rindt drove the Le Mans-winning NART 250 LM to 1st place at Zeltweg, Austria.

David Piper and Dick Attwood won the 9-Hour Endurance Race at Kyalami, South Africa in a 365 P, Peter Sutcliffe and Innes Ireland were 2nd in a Ford GT-40 and 3rd place went to Paul Hawkins and Jackie Epstein in a 250 LM.

The 1965 season ended with the Angola, Italy GP, in which Ferraris were 1st (David Piper—365 P2), 2nd (Muller) and 3rd (Wilson). Ferrari had won the Prototype Trophy and the *Challenge Mondial de Vitesse et d'Endurance.*

The 1966 season opened at Daytona on February 4–5 with the 1st running of the 24 Hours of Daytona. No Ferrari team cars were entered, but many privately entered Ferraris appeared—none of which did particularly well.

The best-placed Ferrari was the NART 365 P2 in 4th place. Three 250 LMs finished 9th (Rindt/Bondurant), 13th (Clarke/Koenig/Hurt) and 15th (Piper/Attwood).

On February 19, 1966, the Ferrari 250 LM berlinetta was homologated as a gran turismo car, two years after Ferrari had requested that status.

The newly homologated 250 LM didn't do well the rest of the season until August 29, when David Piper won the British Eagle Trophy at Brands Hatch. He then won at Oulton Park in a 250 LM and again he, with Dick Attwood, won the Kyalami 9-Hour Race, November 5, in his 365 P2/3. Clarke and Fielding were 2nd in a 250 LM.

Ferraris continued to do well in 1967; 1st, 2nd and 3rd at Daytona (330 P4s), 1st and 2nd at the Monza, Italy 1000-km (330 P4s), 1st at Silverstone (Piper-250 LM), 3rd at Spa-Francorchamps, Belgium (330 P3/4), 2nd at Le Mans (P4), 3rd at Brands Hatch (P4).

By 1968, the 250 LM was really not competitive and the factory no longer campaigned them, but private entrants continued and were reasonably placed in some key events—Rodriguez/Pierpoint 5th at Brands Hatch and Piper/Attwood 7th at Le Mans.

The 250/275 LM had speed, stamina and reliability, but was superseded by more competitive designs.

330 LMB

During the late Fifties and early Sixties, Ferrari had achieved tremendous success with his 3 liter V-12s in both open and closed form. The 250 Testa Rossa was occasionally, but never consistently, beaten by Aston Martin, Maserati or Porsche. The 250 GT berlinetta in both long and short wheelbase versions, while not always victorious, was usually in the winner's circle and quite often one model or a combination would make a sweep of the first five or six places.

In spite of Enzo Ferrari's belief in GT racing, and the 3 liter limit, in 1962, he built two 4 liter prototypes—an open car based on the TRI/61 (which subsequently won the 1962 Le Mans race driven by Hill/Gendebien) and a "GTO" which retired from the same race because of overheating after Parkes deposited the car in the sand bank at Mulsanne while leading the first lap.

Ferrari was obviously trying to hedge his bets as he could not know at this time what the usually capricious CSI would do for the 1963 season. At Ferrari's annual press conference, held in Modena on Dec. 1, 1962, he had no 1963 competition cars to show, and stated that "few if any [more] GTOs would be built" even if the CSI did approve them as legal GT cars "because they were too fast for all but a few first-line drivers."

The 250 GTO berlinetta was the crowning success of the 250 GT series, and while competitors grumbled that the GTO was a race car with a roof on it, the Commission Sportive Internationale of the FIA reaffirmed (on Jan. 29, 1963) that the GTO qualified as a group III GT car.

Ferrari held a second press conference, at the Monza Autodrome, in March, 1963, to introduce his 1963 competition cars; a 3-liter prototype—the mid-engined 250 P, and 4 liter prototype, front-engined coupe called the 330 LM. The designation was subsequently changed to 330 LMB to distinguish it from the 250/275 LM. There was no GTO shown, although GTOs were built in limited quantities through 1964.

The 330 LMB was a sleek-looking, purposeful car which has generally been described as a 250 GT berlinetta Lusso with a GTO nose. Specifications belie this, and it is now generally conceded that

the LMB was actually the work of the Ferrari engineering department, executed by Scaglietti.

The 330 LMB did share design features with both GTO and Lusso, but had its own unmistakable character as a result. The elliptical front air inlet with three "fingernail" shaped supplemental inlets above, and three vertical slot outlets on the flanks of the front fenders displayed its GTO heritage, while the cab—windshield, side and back windows—proclaimed Lusso. Differing from both, however, was the absence of any hood bulge or scoop, the recessed door handles, and the added rear tire clearance by horizontal "tunnels" characteristic of the 1953 250 and 375 MM berlinettas.

Round driving lights, recessed and faired in with clear plastic covers, and air inlets for front brake cooling flanked the eliptical radiator air inlet. Just in front of the hood was a flap to allow access

Above, the 250 LMB, Serial No. 4713, shared the 330 body but the chassis was shorter, with 2400mm (94.5 in) wheelbase. Opposite page. A week before Le Mans, Mike Parkes took Pete Coltrin along for a test ride in the Sears/ Salmon 330 and saw 177 mph at 7100 rpm on the Autostrada between Modena and Bologna.

to the radiator cap without raising the hood (photos show 330 LMB carrying race No. 11 at Le Mans with this flap open). Both car 11 (Gurney/Hall) which was left hand drive, and car 12 (Sears/Salmon), right hand drive, had clear plastic bug deflectors attached to the hood in front of the driver.

Air outlet slots were incorporated into the rear fenders aft of the wheel arch, and while there was no rear spoiler, as such, the body had a definite lip at the upper rear. From some angles, the 330 LMB appears to be a "notchback" design, while from others it resembles the "fastback" Lusso. Under the attractive bodywork the LMB reflected more 400 Superamerica than Lusso.

Front suspension was independent with unequal-length A-arms, coil springs and tubular shocks, augmented by an anti-roll bar. A live rear axle and semi-elliptic springs were used at the rear, with axle control by twin, parallel trailing arms on each side and tubular shocks with concentric coil "compensator" springs. Dunlop disc brakes were used on all four wheels.

The wheelbase, at 2500mm (98.4 inches) was longer than the GTO and the production Lusso at 2400mm (94.5 inches). The engine, as in the 1962 prototypes, was based on the 400 Superamerica with single overhead camshafts, single sparkplug per cylinder, and a bore and stroke of 77 x 71mm for a displacement of 3967cc.

Carburetion was similar to the Testa Rossa and GTO engines, but with larger carburetors—six 42 DCN twin-choke Webers. With a power rating of 400 @ 7500 rpm, it seems likely that cam design might also have been similar to GTO or TR, rather than 400 SA.

A 330 LMB was entered at Sebring on March 23, 1963, for Parkes and Bandini—the first competition appearance for the model. The car was off the course several times, suggesting that either handling or brakes were not yet sorted out. Parkes then slid on a slick spot and hit a tree, splitting the fuel tank, which retired the car on lap 72.

At the traditional Le Mans practice session, held in April, Parkes posted the fifth fastest lap time in a 330 LMB (3 min. 51.4 sec.)—

beaten only by other Ferrari team drivers in the 250 P. Seven Ferrari drivers, four in the 250 P and three in the 330 LMB had bettered Phil Hill's 1962 lap record (3 min. 57.3 sec.) in the winning 4 liter TRI/62.

When the 24 Hours of Le Mans was staged June 15–16, 1963, there were three 330 LMBs and a 250 LMB. The race was a Ferrari benefit, but the best placed LMB was the Sears/Salmon 4 liter car in 5th place, followed by the NART-entered Gregory/Piper 250 LMB in 6th

330 LMB

1/24 scale drawing based on Ferrari No. 4619

ENGINE

Type ....Lampredi-based, water-cooled, 60 degree V-12
Bore/stroke, mm/inches 77.0/71.0, 3.05/2.81
Displacement, cc/cubic inches 3967/242.0
Valve operation: Single overhead camshaft on each bank with roller followers and rocker arms to inclined valves
Valve springs ....Coil
Camshaft drive ....Chain
Ignition ....Two Marelli distributors
Sparkplugs/cyl ....One
Compression ratio 9.0:1
Carburetion ....Six Weber 42 DCN twin-choke, downdraft
BHP (Mfg.) ....400 @ 7500 rpm

DRIVE TRAIN

Clutch ....Single dry-plate
Transmission: Four-speed, all sychromesh, direct drive in 4th gear
Rear axle ....Live
Axle ratios 3.67, 3.78, 4.00, 4.25, 4.55, 4.57, 4.86:1

CHASSIS

Frame ....Welded tubular steel
Wheelbase, mm/inches 2500/98.4
Track, front, mm/inches 1422/56.0
    rear, mm/inches 1414/55.7
Front suspension: Independent, unequal-length A-arms, coil springs
Rear suspension: Live axle, semi-elliptic springs and parallel trailing arms on each side
Shock absorbers ....Tubular
Brakes ....Disc
Tire size, front/rear ....6.00/7.00 x 15
Wheels ....Borrani wire, center-lock, knock-off

GENERAL

Length overall, mm/inches 4485/176.6
Width 1750/68.9
Height 1275/50.2
Body builder ....Scaglietti (Factory design)

place. The Gurney/Hall 330 went out with a broken axle while running 3rd in the 10th hour, and the Noblet/Guichet 330 dropped out after six hours with a loose oil filter.

In August, 1963, Lorenzo Bandini drove a 330 LMB to 3rd overall, in the Guards International Trophy Race at Brands Hatch, England, winning the over 3 liter sports and GT class by beating a D-type Jaguar and a Maserati Tipo 151.

The 250 LMB was entered in the 1963 Tour de France for Jo Schlesser and Claude Leguezec. During the tour, Schlesser won a hill climb, was 4th at the Nurburgring, and 1st at Spa, then over-revved the engine at Reims (9400 on the tell-tale) causing a delay of almost 1½ hours to replace a valve spring. The car was eventually disqualified when the drivers failed to obtain two signatures at Tour checkpoints.

On Feb. 16, 1964, the 250 LMB, still owned by NART, finished 3rd at Daytona (Hansgen/Grossman), then was 15th overall at Sebring (Grossman/Thompson). Grossman bought the car and drove it in the 2-heat Players 200 at Mosport on June 6, 1964, finishing 10th overall and 2nd in GT.

This marked the end of international competition for the 330/250 LMB as Ferrari was concentrating totally on mid-engined competition cars, and would not build another front-engined prototype.

Later, 275 GTB and GTB/Cs, and the 365 GTB/4 "Daytona" would be raced, but these were created as customer "street GTs", not as competition cars, and required considerable modifying to be competitive with contemporary cars.

330 P2/3/4

The Ferrari mid-engined competition sports and prototype cars, both open and closed, started with and developed from the 246 SP in 1961 and progressed through many variants of V-6 and V-8 to the 7-liter V-12s.

The engines were originally 2-cam designs (one overhead camshaft per bank of cylinders), from the 250 Testa Rossa, although competition 250 LMs—starting with the second LM built—had 3.3 liter engines. In 1965 Ferrari returned to a dohc V-12 design with four camshafts, as he had done in 1957 with the 315 and 335 S.

This 1965 car, the P2, utilized features from the Ferrari GP car, including a semi-monocoque chassis. The independent rear suspension had a single transverse locating arm (with the axle shaft it made a parallelogram) and two long radius rods on each side. The dohc V-12 engine had dual ignition and produced 410 bhp at 8200 rpm.

A bewildering array of Ferrari prototype and sports racing cars was fielded in 1965—275 P2 and 330 P2 4-cam cars entered by the factory, and 330 P, 365 P and 365 P2 single-cam cars from private entrants.

A berlinetta version of the P2/3 was tested by John Surtees at Modena in March, 1966, and the car made its racing debut at the Monza 1000-km race in April, 1966. Surtees, making his first racing appearance since his crash at Mosport, Canada, the previous year, teamed with Mike Parkes to win the rain-drenched event.

The Surtees/Parkes car was a 330 P3 and their race average was 103.1 mph with the fastest single lap of the race at 109.2 mph. Both the P3 and the Dinos were plagued by wiper problems and the P3's wipers failed completely on the 30th lap of the race.

Le Mans test day, 1967. Mike Parkes/Lodovico Scarfiotti P4 which later won its class and finished 2nd behind the Foyt/Gurney Ford in the 24 hour classic. Above, business end of a P4 with four camshafts, four coils and two distributors, 5-speed transmission and a lot of wires and plumbing.

March, 1966. John Surtees tests the P3 at Modena. In April the car made its racing debut at the Monza 1000km race and finished 1st in the rain-drenched event, driven by Surtees and Parkes. Bottom. The only berlinettas built on the P2 chassis were for Luigi Chinetti's North American Racing Team.

Cockpit and engine room of P3. Shift lever to 5-speed, rear-mounted transmission is at driver's right. Disc brakes are inboard at the rear.

The P3 was substantially the same as the P2 but the frame had been altered to accommodate wider wheels (8.5 inch front, 9.5 inch rear) and the track width was increased by six centimeters (2.3 inches). Suspension geometry was also altered to suit the wider tires. Lucas fuel injection was now used on the engine and with 10.5:1 compression ratio the horsepower was 420 at 8200 rpm.

A 5-speed ZF transmission was used and the multi-disc clutch was mounted between the engine and gearbox (on the P2 the clutch was behind the transmission). The 330 P3 also marked the first use by Ferrari of fiberglass body panels, although the major portion of the body was still aluminum.

A 330 P berlinetta scored an astounding victory at the Spa-Francorchamps 1000-km race on May 22, 1966. Mike Parkes and Lodovico Scarfiotti, running on Firestone tires for the first time, won

Le Mans, 1967. Willy Mairesse/Jean Beurlys finished 3rd in the Equipe National Belge P4. Opposite page, the Herbert Muller/Jean Guichet Scuderia Filipinetti P3/4 led the Targa Florio until the seventh lap (of 10) when it dropped out with a broken wheel and damaged transaxle.

at an average speed of 131.7 mph and set an absolute lap record of 139 mph.

At Le Mans, on June 18–19, 1966, Ferrari entered three 330 P3s, a spyder for Pedro Rodriguez/Richie Ginther (actually entered by Luigi Chinetti's North American Racing Team), and berlinettas for Parkes/Scarfiotti and Lorenzo Bandini/Jean Guichet. Chinetti also entered a 365 P2 berlinetta, rebodied by Drogo, for Masten Gregory/Bob Bondurant.

The race was a disaster for Ferrari. Labor troubles prevented proper preparation of his cars, and the P3 berlinettas hadn't been touched since their last race. Then Surtees quarreled with Ferrari racing manager Eugenio Dragoni over Scarfiotti being listed as third driver for himself and Parkes, which resulted in Surtees quitting the team. This was actually the final straw in a long-standing battle between Dragoni and Surtees over team structure—Surtees feeling that Dragoni circumvented him in favor of Italian drivers.

All three Dinos and the David Piper/Dick Attwood 365 P2/3 went out in the third hour. Scarfiotti crashed the 330 P berlinetta in the ninth hour while in 2nd place. The NART 365 P2 berlinetta went out an hour later with gearbox troubles.

In the 11th hour the Rodriguez/Ginther 330 P3 retired when the shift mechanism failed. An hour later the Mairesse/Muller 365 P2/3 went out with transmission problems, and two hours later the Ecurie Francorchamps 365 P2/3 blew a head gasket. In the early morning hours the Bandini/Guichet 330 P berlinetta, already plagued by a slipping clutch, blew a head gasket and retired.

At the end of the 24-hour event, won by Ford, only two Ferraris were running; the Pike/Courage GTB which finished 1st in GT and 8th overall, and the Noblet/DuBois GTB which finished 10th overall.

Ferrari 330 berlinettas did little for the rest of the 1966 season, and some cars were sold to private customers. These had even wider wheels (11.5-inch front and rear) which required chassis modifications to accommodate them.

On December 12, 1966, a Ferrari 330 P4 was taken to Daytona for trials on Firestone tires which Ferrari was contracted to use during the 1967 season.

In addition to chassis changes to accept the wider tires (10.15 x 15 front/12.15 x 15 rear on 9.5- and 11.5-inch rims) and a still wider track, a Ferrari-designed and built transmission replaced the ZF unit. A new engine, designed by engineer Rocchi was being tested. This was a 36-valve V-12 with two intake valves and one exhaust valve per cylinder. The Lucas fuel injection fed into induction tubes between the camshafts instead of on the inside of the cylinder banks as on previous Ferrari V-12 engine designs.

Two sparkplugs (reduced from 12 to 10mm) per cylinder and four coils were used and, with its 11.0:1 compression ratio, the engine was rated at 450 bhp at 8200 rpm. This engine was developed from the Formula 1 Ferraris that ran at Monza. The test drivers—Parkes, Scarfiotti, Bandini and Chris Amon—drove a total of 580 laps and reportedly topped 210 mph.

When the cars appeared at the Daytona Continental on February 4–5, 1967, the test spyder was driven by Amon and Bandini, and a new berlinetta was entered for Scarfiotti and Parkes. NART entered a P3, brought up to P4 specifications, for Pedro Rodriguez and Jean Guichet. This car was equipped with carburetors instead of fuel injection. A similar 330 P3/4 was entered by Ecurie Francorchamps for Mairesse/Beurlys, David Piper drove his own 330 P2/3 and NART entered the Drogo-bodied 365 P2 streamliner for Masten Gregory and Jo Schlesser.

The Ferraris had minor difficulties during the race—Bandini's car needed front wheel balancing, the Parkes car had the front brake pads changed, and Rodriguez' shift linkage had to be repaired, but just before the finish the Amon/Bandini, Parkes/Scarfiotti, and Rodriguez/Guichet Ferraris lined up to cross the finish line abreast. This was obviously a dig at Ford for the 1966 Le Mans race finish.

On April 25, 1967, at the Monza 1000-km race, Ferrari 330 P4

A P 4 in the paddock at Monza and opposite page, the Beurlys/Mairesse 3rd place P 4 at Le Mans in 1967.

berlinettas finished 1st (Bandini/Amon), 2nd (Parkes/Scarfiotti) and 4th (Nino Vaccarella/Herbert Muller).

The Spa-Francorchamps 1000 km race, on May 1, was not an auspicious event for Ferrari. Two 330 P3/4 berlinettas were entered, by Equipe National Belge for Willy Mairesse, and Maranello Concessionaires for Dick Attwood/Lucien Bianchi, and a factory P3/4 for Parkes/Scarfiotti.

At the finish it was a Mirage, Porsche 910, the Attwood/Bianchi P3/4, a Lola, and in 5th, the Parkes/Scarfiotti P4. The 3rd place Ferrari did get four points toward the manufacturer's championship for Ferrari.

May 14, at the 51st Targa Florio, Ferrari entered a 330 P4 spyder for Vaccarella and Scarfiotti. Scuderia Filipinetti entered a 330 P3/4 berlinetta for Muller and Guichet, and a 330 LM for Heini Walter and Gottfried Kochert.

The Targa Florio—10 laps of a 44.7-mile circuit through the

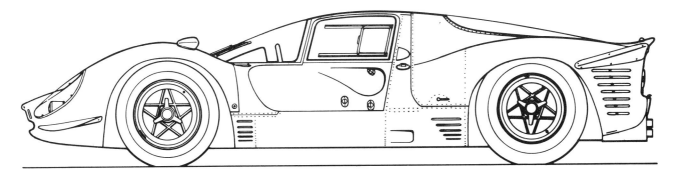

330 P2/3/4

1/24 scale drawing based on Ferrari No. 0858

ENGINE

Type ....Rocchi-designed, water-cooled, 60 degree V-12
Bore/stroke, mm/inches 77.0/71.0, 3.05/2.81
Displacement, cc/cubic inches 3967/242.0
Valve operation: Double overhead camshafts on each bank
Valve springs ....Coil
Camshaft drive...Chain
Ignition ....Two Marelli distributors
Sparkplugs/cyl ....Two
Compression ratio 11.0:1
Carburetion ....Lucas fuel injection
BHP (Mfg.) ....450 @ 8000 rpm

DRIVE TRAIN

Clutch ....Single dry-plate
Transmission: Five-speed, all synchromesh, direct drive in 5th
    gear
Rear axle ....Transaxle with halfshafts
Axle ratios ....Various, data not available

CHASSIS

Frame ....Tubular steel with aluminum skin
Wheelbase, mm/inches 2400/94.5
Track, front, mm/inches 1488/58.6
    rear, mm/inches...1450/57.1
Front suspension: Independent, unequal-length A-arms, coil springs
Rear suspension: Independent, unequal-length upper and lower arms,
    coil springs
Shock absorbers...Tubular
Brakes ....Disc
Tire size, front/rear...................................4.75–10.30/6.00–12.30 x 15
Wheels...................................Campagnolo alloy, center-lock, knock-off

GENERAL

Length overall, mm/inches 4185/164.8
Width 1810/71.3
Height...1000/39.4
Body builder ....Drogo (Factory design)

mountains of Sicily—is a difficult race to finish, let alone do well in. On the second lap, Gunther Klass hit a marker stone, eliminating his Dino. Then 1965 Targa-winner Vaccarella made a rare mistake, misjudging his speed in his home town of Collesano, and hit a wall, breaking both right wheels. Both of Ferrari's best team cars were now out.

Scuderia Filipinetti's 330 P3/4 got the lead back for Ferrari but came into the pits on the seventh lap with a broken wheel and a damaged transaxle. Porsche finished 1st, 2nd and 3rd, with a two-year-old Dino (Venturi/Williams) in 4th, giving three more points to Ferrari toward the championship.

No Ferrari team cars were entered at the 1000 km of Nurburgring as Ferrari was saving his big effort for Le Mans, two weeks later.

Four 330 P4s appeared at Le Mans; berlinettas for Parkes/Scarfiotti, and Gunther Klass/Peter Sutcliffe, and spyders for Amon/Vaccarella and Mairesse/Beurlys in the Equipe National Belge entry. All four cars were equipped with the 36-valve, 4-cam, Lucas-Injected V-12s and Ferrari-designed 5-speed transmissions. The gearbox cases were of magnesium which saved 30 lbs over the aluminum cases.

NART, Maranello Concessionaires and Scuderia Filipinetti entered the same 330 P3/4s they had raced all season, but with the new Ferrari-designed 5-speed transmissions. Pedro Rodriguez/Giancarlo Baghetti drove for NART, Dick Attwood/Piers Courage for Maranello Concessionaires, and Muller/Guichet for Filipinetti. The NART 365 P2/3 long-tailed berlinetta was entered for Chuck Parsons/Ricardo Rodriguez (this Ricardo was not related to Pedro Rodriguez).

The race started out as a Ford-Chaparral duel and by midnight, eight hours after the start, two Ferraris were out (the NART 365 P/2 in the sand at Mulsanne, and the Filipinetti P3/4 with a broken piston), the Parkes/Scarfiotti P4 was in 3rd behind the Gurney/Foyt and McLaren/Donohue Fords, and the leaders were averaging 140 mph.

At 1:00 a.m. the Gurney, McLaren and Andretti Fords and the Scarfiotti Ferrari were on the same lap. At 2:00 a.m. Rodriguez' Ferrari went out with a blown engine, then the brakes locked on Andretti's Ford as he went through the esses and McCluskey and Schlesser crashed avoiding Mario, leaving Fords all over the course. About this time the Maranello Concessionaires' P3/4 went out with a broken oil pump drive.

The Foyt/Gurney Ford had a long lead with Parkes/Scarfiotti in 2nd and the Chaparral 3rd but the latter dropped out about 5:00 a.m. with the transmission oil seal gone.

With two hours to go, the Ferraris started to close the gap and were gaining about 10 seconds a lap on the Fords but Foyt and Gurney were driving fast enough to maintain the lead—and they made no mistakes. Mike Parkes later told Paul Frere "never in my life have I driven a car so hard for so long."

The Le Mans timers, located just before the shut-off point on the Mulsanne straight, recorded all the Fords at over 200 mph with the Andretti/Bianchi car fastest at 213; the Chaparral at an even 200, the Surtees/Hobbs Lola-Aston Martin at 205 mph. The fastest Ferrari was the Parkes/Scarfiotti P4 at 193 mph.

Ford's 1st place gave the make nine points, Ferrari's 2nd received six, and the 5th place Porsche got two. The Manufacturer's Championship now stood at 32 points for Porsche and 31 for Ferrari.

The Manufacturer's Championship would be decided at the BOAC 500 at Brands Hatch on July 30. The Phil Hill/Mike Spence Chaparral won, but the Chris Amon/Jackie Stewart Ferrari 330 P4 was 2nd, giving Ferrari the championship with 34 points. Porsche ended the season with 32, and Ford had 22 points. This was the twelfth time in 14 years that Ferrari won the Manufacturer's Championship.

Thus ended the competition career of the berlinetta developed from the 246 SP V-6.

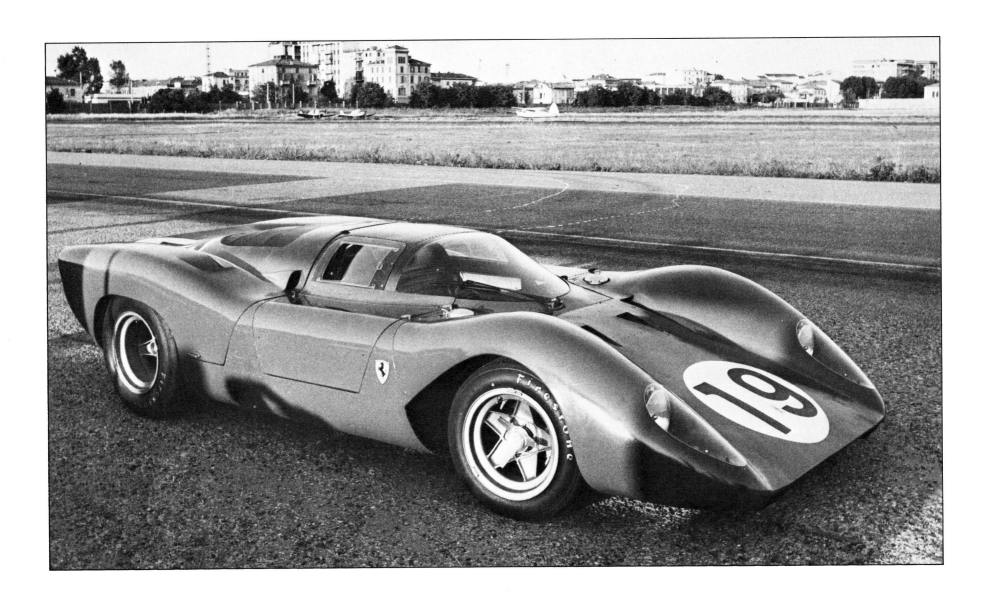

312 P

At the end of the 1968 season Ferrari engineers Calari (aerodynamics), Rocchi (engines) and Marelli (development) under the capable direction of Mauro Forghieri were completing the new 312 Prototype to run in the 1969 Manufacturers Championship series.

The 312 P had a 48-valve, 60-degree, V-12 engine with 77 x 53.5mm bore and stroke. Displacing 2990cc it was developed from the Formula 1 engine. With 11.0:1 compression ratio, single Marelli distributor and Lucas fuel injection the power rating was 430 at 9800 rpm.

Resembling a scaled-down Can-Am car, the 312 P had a shorter wheelbase (93.3 inches), was narrower (77.9 inches) and lighter (1496 pounds). In addition, the 312 P had headlights, which were required on Prototype cars, and did not have the wing and air brake of the 612 Can-Am.

Front suspension was independent with upper and lower A-arms, concentric coil spring/shock absorbers and an anti-roll bar. Rear suspension also was independent with single upper arm and reversed lower A-arm, radius rods, concentric coil spring/shock absorbers and anti-roll bar.

Like the 612, the 312 P had outboard-mounted Girling disc brakes, but unlike the 612, had a 5-speed instead of a 4-speed transmission.

Mauro Forghieri had been promoted from Race Manager to Chief Engineer, his place in the field being taken by Stefano Jacoponi, and drivers for 1969 were Chris Amon, Derek Bell, and Tino Brambilla. Peter Schetty and Gianclaudio "Clay" Regazzoni had also signed with Ferrari, Mario Andretti was available for Prototype races that didn't conflict with his USAC schedule, and Mike Parkes was back

A berlinetta version of the 312 P was tested at Modena for the 1969 Le Mans race where two were entered for Amon/Schetty and Rodriguez/Piper. Neither car finished.

performing his engineering duties but was not expected to drive for awhile.

The new 312 P was damaged during testing at Vallelunga, with Brambilla driving, and missed the Daytona 24-hour race in February 1961. Its first outing was in the Sebring 12-hour event where it finished 2nd, driven by Amon and Andretti. Then it finished 4th in the Brands Hatch, England 500. Two 312 Ps entered in the Monza 1000-km race retired—one with no oil pressure, and one in an accident.

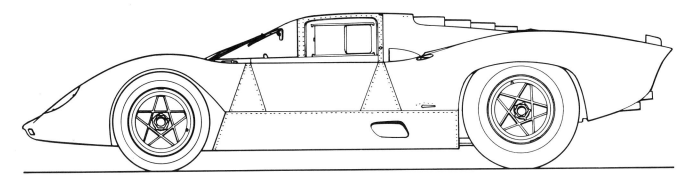

312 P

1/24 scale drawing based on Ferrari No. 0870

ENGINE

Type ....Forghieri/Rocchi-designed, water-cooled 60 degree V-12
Bore/stroke, mm/inches 77.0/53.5, 3.05/2.12
Displacement, cc/cubic inches.............................2990/182.4
Valve operation: Double overhead camshafts on each bank
Valve springs ....Coil
Camshaft drive..Chain
Ignition ....Two Marelli distributors
Sparkplugs/cyl ....One
Compression ratio 11.0:1
Carburetion ....Lucas fuel injection
BHP (Mfg.) ....430 @ 9800 rpm

DRIVE TRAIN

Clutch ....Single dry-plate
Transmission: Five-speed, all synchromesh, direct drive in 5th
    gear
Rear axle ....Transaxle with halfshafts
Axle ratios ....Various, data not available

CHASSIS

Frame ....Tubular steel with aluminum skin
Wheelbase, mm/inches 2370/93.3
Track, front, mm/inches 1485/58.5
    rear, mm/inches...1500/59.1
Front suspension: Independent, unequal-length A-arms, coil
    springs
Rear suspension: Independent, unequal-length upper and lower
    arms, coil springs
Shock absorbers..Tubular
Brakes ....Disc
Tire size, front/rear....................4.75–10.30/6.00–13.50 x 15
Wheels..................................Campagnolo alloy, center-lock, knock-off

GENERAL

Length overall, mm/inches 4230/166.5
Width 1980/77.9
Height...950/37.4
Body builder ....Drogo (Factory design)

Ferrari skipped the Targa Florio but sent one 312 P to Spa-Francorchamps, Belgium, where Rodriguez/Piper finished 2nd. One car again went to the Nurburgring 1000-km race in Germany and after a see-saw battle with the Porsche 908, the Amon/Rodriguez 312 P dropped out with ignition failure.

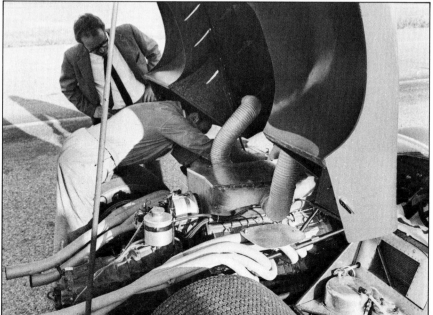

A berlinetta version of the 312 P* was being tested by Ferrari and two of the new cars were entered at Le Mans, in June, 1969, to be driven by Amon/Schetty and Rodriguez/Piper. After removing some experimental tabs from the nose, and a spoiler from the tail, Rodriguez got down to a lap time of 3 minutes, 35.5 seconds, and Amon was only one-tenth second slower.

Even though the Ferraris were two of the faster cars in the race, they were destined to fail. On the first lap Amon had the misfortune to run over the wreckage of a Porsche 917 that crashed just ahead of him, and was out of the race because of damage to the undercarriage of his Ferrari. The Rodriguez/Piper 312 P berlinetta ran in the top 10 until the 13th hour when it went out with gearbox problems.

The 312 P contested six races in 1969 and in every event it started in the pole position, led the race or challenged the leaders and yet, with eight entries in six races, could do no better than two 2nds and one 4th place.

At the 1970 season opener, at Daytona, five Ferrari 512s were entered plus two NART 312 P berlinettas for Adamowicz/Piper and Parkes/Posey, who finished respectively in 4th and 5th places.

The 312 Ps, in both spyder and berlinetta form, were campaigned by private entrants during 1970 and 1971 seasons, with varying success. But the advent of the 312 PB, with its 180-degree opposed, 4-cam, 12-cylinder engine rendered the older V-12 obsolete. The 312 PB ran only in spyder form as no berlinettas were built.

At Daytona in 1971, one of the NART 312 P V-12 berlinettas appeared with spyder bodywork and, driven by Coco Chinetti and Garcia Veiga, finished 5th.

Once again, Ferrari's forces had been divided—this time between the 312 P and the 512 S and M—to the detriment of both. The Ferrari organization, which built such magnificent racing machines, often was its own worst enemy.

*Only two 312 P chassis were built and ran at various times with spyder or berlinetta bodywork.

512 S & M

A Pininfarina berlinetta *speciale* Ferrari on a 512 chassis was shown at Turin in November, 1969. It was strictly a show car with a windshield that was almost horizontal (12 degree slope) and rear fenders that rose gradually from a point just behind the front wheels to a sharply truncated rear end. It was an impractical design from a useful standpoint, but as a show car it was magnificent.

In March, 1970, at the Geneva show, Pininfarina presented another 512 S—the *Modulo*. It was only 36.8 inches high and the roof section (including the side windows) slid forward for entry. A horizontal bumper-like band encircled the car and the tops of the wheels were left exposed. It was a superb design exercise but once again served little purpose other than as an attention-getting creation.

A 512 S competition car was shown at Ferrari's press conference at Maranello in December, 1969. It was a purposeful, aggressive-looking machine—totally unlike the two show cars. Under the body it was similar to the 312 P and 612 Can Am cars with its 94.4 inch-wheelbase and tubular frame with riveted body panels, by Cigarla & Bertinetti of Turin.

The 60 degree, d.o.h.c. V-12 engine had 87 x 70mm bore and stroke with a displacement of 4994cc, Lucas indirect fuel injection and 48 valves. The compression ratio was 11.8:1, a single Marelli distributor was used and horsepower was 550 at 8500 rpm. The 512 weighed 1850 pounds and maximum speed was reported to be 218 mph in 5th gear.

Front suspension was independent with upper and lower A-arms, concentric coil springs and tubular shock absorbers and an anti-roll bar. The rear suspension was also independent but with single upper arms and reversed lower A-arms with concentric coil springs, tubular shock absorbers, and anti-roll bar.

Opposite page. Jacky Ickx/John Surtees 512 S was 2nd at 1970 Spa-Francorchamps 1000km race. Below, cockpit of 512 S—12,000 rpm tach in front of driver, gated shift lever to his right.

Pininfarina 512 S berlinetta Speciale was shown at the Turin Show in November, 1969. Opposite page, the competition 512 S carried its required spare wheel & tire under the

removable number plate panel. High tail and low roof, with minimal slope, made louvered rear window necessary for maximum rear vision with lack of distortion.

The 5-speed, all-synchromesh gearbox was in unit with the limited slip differential. Girling ventilated disc brakes were used all around. Water radiators were on either side of the engine and the oil coolers were in the nose.

Ferrari planned to field three cars for major events of 1970 with Jacky Ickx, Peter Schetty, Arturo Merzario, Tino Brambilla, Ignazio Giunti, Nino Vaccarella and, when available, Mario Andretti as drivers.

To qualify for the 5 liter Group 5 Sports Car category, 25 cars had to be built. Ferrari completed the required amount by the end of the 1969 season and while a few were made available to private teams, most remained at the factory for development and for spare parts.

During the 1970 season both spyder and berlinetta 512 S Ferraris were seen in competition.

Daytona, January 31, was not a "Ferrari race" with Gulf Porsches 1st and 2nd and Ferrari 512 S in 3rd (Andretti/Merzario/Ickx), 4th (Parkes/Posey) and 5th (Piper/Adamowicz).

Ferrari fortunes were better at Sebring, March 21, with the Andretti/Giunti/Vaccarella 512 S berlinetta 1st. Parkes and Parsons were 6th in a 312 P, and all the other Ferraris dropped out. The Andretti/Merzario and Bucknum/Posey 512s were spyders while the Ickx/Schetty 512 S was a berlinetta like the winner.

The Sebring cars had modifications to the fuel injection that increased horsepower by 40, and chassis changes that reduced weight by 80 pounds.

Three Ferrari factory entries appeared at Monza for the 1000 km race; Amon/Merzario and Schetty/Surtees in 512 S berlinettas and Giunti/Vaccarella in a 512 S spyder. The team entries all finished, but in 2nd, 3rd and 4th places behind the Gulf Porsche.

The Ickx/Surtees 512 S berlinetta finished 2nd at the Spa-Francorchamps 1000 km race and a strong drive by Ickx brought them within three minutes of the winning Porsche.

At the Nurburgring, Surtees/Vaccarella were 3rd in a 512 S spyder and Muller/Parkes finished 4th in a 512 S berlinetta behind a pair of 908/3 Porsches.

Finishing off a poor season for Ferrari was the Le Mans debacle. Eight 512 S berlinettas with the *coda lunga* (long tail) bodies were entered—factory entries for Ickx/Schetty, Merzario/Regazzoni, Giunti/Vaccarella and Bell/Peterson; Scuderia Filipinetti entries for Parkes/Muller and Bonnier/Wisell; a NART car for Posey/Bucknum and a Belgian entry for De Fierlandt/Walker.

Private 512 S berlinettas, in the standard body configuration were entered for Loos/Kelleners, Juncadella/Fernandez and Moretti/Manfredini, and NART brought a 312 P berlinetta for Adamowicz/Parsons. An extremely strong field of twelve Ferrari berlinettas that should have, on specification, dominated the race.

During the rain that fell early in the event, Reine Wisell slowed his 512 because of poor visibility due to oil on the windshield and was hit by Regazzoni, and then Parkes. Bell overturned his 512 in the confusion, and four Ferraris were out of the race.

The Giunti/Vaccarella 512 went out with engine failure, the Loos/Kelleners 512 retired with a damaged nose, and the Moretti/Manfredini 512 went into the *parc ferme* with a dry gearbox.

Ickx and Schetty were running 3rd after nine hours—the only Ferrari with a chance of winning—when a rear brake locked putting

Opposite, top, 512 S Coda Lunga (long tail) during tests at Modena and below, the Sam Posey/Ron Bucknum 4th place Coda Lunga NART entry at Le Mans in 1970. Opposite, below, a 512 goes through Campofelice in the Targa Florio.

Ickx off the track, killing a course marshal. The car burst into flames and was partially destroyed. Juncadella's 512 then expired with a split gearbox casing.

Three Ferraris were still running at the end of the 24-Hour race; the Posey/Bucknum entry was 4th, and the de Fierlandt/Walker car was 5th. The Adamowicz 312 P didn't cover enough distance to be classified.

Never one to take defeat easily, whether caused by his opposition or by the failure of his own cars to perform as planned, Ferrari developed the 512 M (for *modificata*) in time for Giunti/Ickx to run at Austria's Osterreichring. The berlinetta bodywork was more aerodynamic and had small adjustable wings at the back and a carburetor airscoop sticking up behind the cockpit roof.

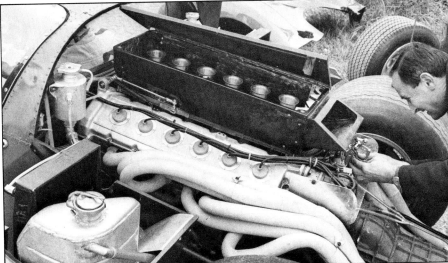

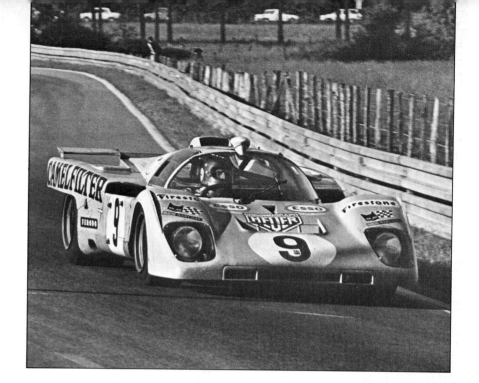

Left, top, the Roger Penske-Kirk White 512 M at Le Mans in 1971 where, driven by Mark Donohue and David Hobbs, it retired with engine trouble while running 4th. Left, below, Scuderia Filipinetti 512 undergoing development by Mike Parkes. Roof bubble is to clear Parkes' helmet. Below, a 512 at Le Mans and right, the inner workings of the Penske 512 M.

The new 512 M easily outdistanced the Porsches early in the race, and set a new lap record, but retired with electrical problems. The 512 M was vindicated at Kyalami, in South Africa, where Ickx and Giunti started on the pole and stayed in front to the finish. Bell and De Fierlandt were 6th in the Belgian-entered 512 S berlinetta.

The 1971 season got off to a tragic start at Buenos Aires with Ignazio Giunti losing his life in a 312 PB. The 512 Ms of Juncadella/Pairetti, Gosselin/DeFierlandt, Parkes/Bonnier and Posey/De Palma/Veiga finished 5th, 6th, 7th and 8th.

Ferrari was directing his factory's efforts to the development of the new 3 liter Group 6 car—the 312 PB with a flat 12 engine derived from the Formula 1 design—so the 512 Ms were campaigned by independent teams with some factory assistance. The fastest of these, the blue and yellow Penske-Sunoco-Kirk White 512 M, ran into a series of unpredictable mishaps.

At Daytona in February 1971, the Penske car, driven by Mark Donohue and David Hobbs, led early in the race, lost some time from electrical problems, then was hit by a Porsche 914. The Ferrari, with its once handsome body taped together, finished 3rd. The Bucknum/Adamowicz NART 512 S was 2nd and an old NART 312 P berlinetta rebodied as a spyder was driven to 5th place by Chinetti/Veiga. The Young/Gregory and Posey/Revson 512 Ms retired.

At Sebring the Penske 512 M once again ran away from the field at the start, but once more a collision with a Porsche (Rodriguez' Gulf 917) ruined any chance of winning and Donohue and Hobbs were 6th.

Muller/Herzog and Juncadella/Hobbs 512 Ms were 4th and 5th at Brands Hatch, England and at Monza, Italy, Muller/Herzog and Moretti/Zeccoli were 6th and 8th. At Spa-Francorchamps in Belgium, the best the 512 Ms could do were 13th (Manfredini and Cagliardi) and 15th (Muller and Herzog).

At Le Mans, in June, there were nine 512 M Ferraris entered for the 1971 24-Hour Race. Donohue and Hobbs were the fastest of the Ferraris but could only run 4th behind the long-tailed Porsches and then retired, after five hours, with engine trouble.

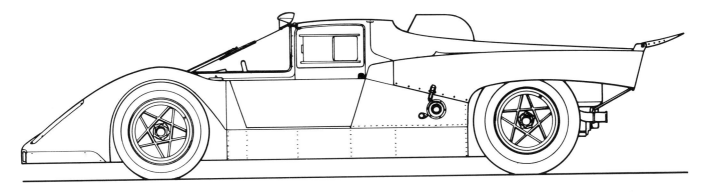

512 M

1/24 scale drawing based on Ferrari No. 1040

ENGINE

Type ....Marelli/Rocchi-designed, water-cooled, 60 degree V-12
Bore/stroke, mm/inches 87.0/70.0, 3.48/2.77
Displacement, cc/cubic inches.................................4994/274.1
Valve operation: Double overhead camshafts on each bank
Valve springs ....Coil
Camshaft drive..Chain
Ignition ....Dinoplex transister
Sparkplugs/cyl ....One
Compression ratio 11.8.1
Carburetion ....Lucas fuel injection
BHP (Mfg.) ....610 @ 9000 rpm

DRIVE TRAIN

Clutch ....Multi-disc
Transmission: Five-speed, all synchromesh, direct drive in 5th
  gear
Rear axle ....Transaxle with halfshafts
Axle ratios 3.18, 3.40, 3.78, 4.25:1

CHASSIS

Frame ....Tubular steel with aluminum skin
Wheelbase, mm/inches 2400/94.5
Track, front, mm/inches 1518/59.8
  rear, mm/inches.......................................1511/59.5
Front suspension: Independent, unequal-length A-arms, coil
  springs
Rear suspension: Independent, unequal-length upper and lower
  arms, coil springs
Shock absorbers...Tubular
Brakes ....Disc
Tire size, front/rear....................4.25–11.50/6.00–14.50 x 15
Wheels ....Campagnolo alloy, center-lock, hex nut

GENERAL

Length overall, mm/inches 4360/171.7
Width 2000/78.7
Height...970/38.2
Body builder ....Drogo (Factory design)

The 512 M at Austria's Osterreichring in 1970. The Jacky Ickx/Ignazio Giunti 512 M at speed, and abandoned (by Ickx) on the course with electrical problems.

At the beginning of the season it was thought that the Ferrari 512 M and the Porsche 917-30 were evenly matched, but Ferrari's attention was focused on the 312 PB Group 6 car. The 512 suffered the obvious results of this inattention and in the final major events of 1971 could do no better than 4th; Pasotti/Casoni at the Osterreichring and De Cadenet/Motschenbacher at Watkins Glen.

At the last championship race for the big group 5 cars, the Watkins Glen 6-Hour, the spectators were treated to a tremendous exhibition of speed with Mark Donohue in the Penske 512 M commanding an early lead. Donohue was almost a lap ahead of the field when a steering arm failed, causing the Ferrari to go off the track.

The Penske-prepared 512 M was one of the fastest racing cars in the world in 1971 and had, in Mark Donohue, one of the best drivers ever to sit behind the wheel of a racing car, but in four races it had the dismal record of two dnfs, one 6th and one 3rd place.

At an *Interserie* race at the Norisring, Pedro Rodriguez put Muller's 512 M into the front row of the grid, next to a 7.6 liter McLaren, and led the first laps. But Pedro crashed into a barrier while avoiding a slower car and lost his life as the car shot across the track in flames.

The 512 S and 512 M did not achieve the success that they should have in 1970 and 1971. This was partly due to the neglect by Ferrari himself, and partly to the strong effort from Porsche with the 917 series.

Charlie Kolb winning the 1965 Nassau Tourist Trophy race in the 275 GTB/C at an average speed of 91.6 mph.

275 GTB/C

Ferrari's 250 GT Lusso was still in production when Pininfarina introduced two new models at the Paris Auto Show in October, 1964; the 275 GTB (berlinetta) and 275 GTS (spyder).

The Lusso was the last in a long line of very successful Ferrari models—both competition and road—based on the conventional chassis layout developed from the early Ferraris (tubular steel, ladder-type frame, front-mounted V-12 engine and transmission, live rear axle with coil front and semi-elliptic rear springs). It was the classic example of the late Laurence Pomeroy's theory, paraphrased, that a well-developed outdated design was probably superior to a newer but untried design that might look better on paper.

The 275 series, introduced in 1965, was the first production Ferrari to have a front-mounted V-12 engine with independent rear suspension. It also had a rear-mounted 5-speed transmission. The Pininfarina-designed bodies were again built by Scaglietti in Modena.

The 275 engine was Ferrari's 60 degree V-12, with a single overhead camshaft on each bank, and displaced 3286cc. The GTS engine, with 9.2:1 compression ratio, was rated at 260 hp at 7000 rpm. Carburetion was by three 40mm Weber carburetors. The GTB, with 9.5:1 compression ratio produced 280 hp at 7500 rpm. A hotter version, with six 40 DCN Webers, developed 300 hp at 7600 rpm.

Drive, on all versions, went through a single dry-plate clutch and an open drive shaft to a 5-speed, all-synchromesh transaxle. Disc brakes were used all around and suspension was independent on all four wheels, with unequal-length A-arms, concentric coil springs and tubular shocks, and anti-roll bars were mounted front and rear.

The 275 GTB had minor changes for 1966—a longer nose, mag wheels and a torque tube driveshaft (the open shaft on the 1965 cars had resulted in bending, misalignment, vibration and often the need to replace shaft and bearings).

Then came Ferrari's first production model with four overhead camshafts; the dohc 275 GTB/4. The engine had six 40 DCN Weber carburetors as standard equipment, but the chassis and body were virtually identical to the 275 GTB. *All* GTBs could be ordered with aluminum-alloy bodies.

An additional version, the 275 GTB/C—for *competizione*—was also built in 1966, and in such limited quantity (probably no more than 20) that even some Ferrari enthusiasts are not aware of the model. Visually similar to other GTBs, it can be identified by the serial number plate in the engine compartment.

The GTB/C had an aluminum-alloy body that had the same shape as the long-nose, two-cam GTBs of that year. Fenders were a bit wider than those of the GTB, the aluminum skin was thinner, and the windows were plastic rather than glass.

Most of the GTB/Cs had the fuel filler inside the trunk, but a few had the filler in the right "sail panel" behind the louvers, and a cover for the oil sump tank filler on the right front fender.

Some "C" models had bumpers, and some did not, and were built both as left and right hand drive. Aside from the obvious United Kingdom buyers who would want right hand drive, this was intended to be a competition car and as most races are run in a clockwise direction, a driver sitting on the right was on the inside of most turns, and was on the pit side of the car which saved valuable time during pit stops.

Three Weber 40 DFI/1 carburetors were standard although six 40 DCN 2 Webers were available as an option. It appears that few cars

were built with six carburetors because FIA rules required the same number of carburetors as the homologated version. Other than carburetion, the engine appears to be identical to the 250 LM engine (which was actually a 275 from the second car on) with its dry-sump lubrication.

Even though visually similar, the GTB/C had different parts numbers from the 1966 standard GTB. The frame did have an extra cross member (under the dry-sump tank), which was the only noticeable difference, and the 5-speed transmission had extra close ratios but externally looked like the standard transmission.

The GTB/C reverted back to the exposed driveshaft of the 1965 GTB. Ed Niles, in a story on the GTB/C in the Ferrari Owners Club publication, expressed the theory that this was to facilitate clutch or gearbox work in a racing pit stop, and he may well be right. There is

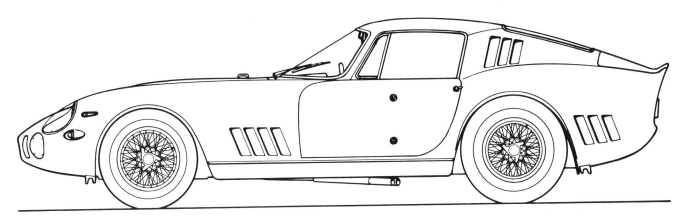

275 GTB/C

1/24 scale drawing based on Ferrari No. 06885

ENGINE

Type ....Columbo-based, water-cooled 60 degree V-12
Bore/stroke, mm/inches 77.0/58.8, 3.05/2.315
Displacement, cc/cubic inches 3286/200.5
Valve operation: Single overhead camshaft on each bank with roller followers and rocker arms to inclined valves
Valve springs ....Coil
Camshaft drive..Chain
Ignition ....Two Marelli distributors
Sparkplugs/cyl ....One
Compression ratio 9.7:1
Carburetion ....Six Weber 40 DCZ6 twin-choke, downdraft
BHP (Mfg.) ....320 @ 7700 rpm

DRIVE TRAIN

Clutch ....Single dry-plate
Transmission: Five-speed, all synchromesh, in unit with differential
Rear axle ....Transaxle with halfshafts
Axle ratios 3.30, 3.50:1

CHASSIS

Frame ....Welded tubular steel
Wheelbase, mm/inches 2400/94.5
Track, front, mm/inches 1377/54.2
    rear, mm/inches 1393/54.8
Front suspension: Independent, unequal-length A-arms, coil springs
Rear suspension: Independent, unequal-length A-arms, coil springs
Shock absorbers...Tubular
Brakes ....Disc
Tire size, front/rear..............................5.50/7.00 x 15
Wheels..................................Borrani wire, center-lock, knock-off

GENERAL

Length overall, mm/inches 4280/168.5
Width 1685/66.3
Height..1350/53.1
Body builder ....Scaglietti (Pininfarina design)

The 275 GTB was seen regularly in private hands at hill climbs— here at Freiburg in 1967. Car No. 24 was driven by Willy Mairesse and Jean Beurlys to 1st in GT and 3rd overall at Le Mans in 1965. The nose was brutally hacked open for cooling.

no other obvious explanation.

Also, three-ear, center-lock knock-on Borrani wire wheels (like those on the 250 LM) were used on some GTB/Cs in contrast to the mag wheels of the *normale* GTB. The wire wheels, like those of the 250 LM, were unusual in that the front wheels (7 x 15) were laced to the outer part of the rim, while the rear wheels (7.5 x 15) were laced to the drop-center of the rim. Some cars had regular 14" alloy wheels.

The *raison d'etre* for the GTB/C isn't totally clear, but it appeared in competition for the first time at the Nurburgring 1000-km race in May, 1965. The car, No. 6885, was driven in practice by Bandini, and was faster than the GTOs, but was driven in the race by Baghetti and Biscaldi—unfortunately with rather mediocre results.

This GTB/C had a Lusso-type hood airscoop/blister covering six dual Webers, and a nose that looked more 330 LMB or 250 GTO than 275 GTB. The rear fenders had three air slots behind the wheel, and the fender-tops swept almost straight back rather than dropping off as in the normal GTB design.

In June the car ran at Le Mans in Scuderia Francorchamps Belgian yellow and, driven by Mairesse and Beurlys, finished 3rd overall and 1st in GT class. Inasmuch as this was during the period when Ferrari was fighting the FIA over homologation of the 250 LM, it must have been a great source of satisfaction for Ferrari.

After being used by the factory, No. 6885 and a similar car, No. 6701, were sold to private parties, and at the end of the season Charlie Kolb drove No. 6885 to victory in the Nassau Tourist Trophy.

The GTB/C conformed to existing FIA rules, which allowed alterations to springs, shock absorbers, brakes, etc., and considerable lightening was done in non-stressed areas. Weight of the GTB/C was quoted at 2112 lbs—compared to the standard GTB with aluminum body at 2420 lbs. Both are figures are questionable as genuine Ferrari weights were seldom as light as factory claims.

Regardless, the GTB/C was a fine addition to the existing line of thoroughbred cars from Maranello and were the last single-cam berlinettas produced. Ferrari experts Ed Niles and Jess Pourret, writing in the Ferrari Owners Club magazine say the "C" is a real sleeper as a collector's car—and they are correct. The "C" is very fast, highly maneuverable and reliable, yet docile and tractable enough to allow normal road use with complete impunity.

365 GTB/4

At the Paris Salon in October, 1968, Ferrari previewed the most expensive, most exotic, and fastest customer production road car in his company's 21-year history; the 365 Gran Turismo Berlinetta with a front-mounted, four overhead-camshaft engine, and 5-speed rear transaxle. The list price was under $20,000 (increased to $25,200 by 1973) and the factory claimed top speed was 174 mph. In a *Road & Track* road test conducted in Nevada in 1970, a Daytona, as the model was now called, achieved an honest 173 mph as a mean average on a two-way run. The tach read 7000 in fifth gear, and the speedometer read 180 mph. And this impressive speed was obtained at an altitude of 4,500 feet above sea level.

Even though debuted at Paris in 1968, real production didn't get underway at Ferrari and Scaglietti, where the bodies were built, until late 1969.

While quite heavy for a GT car, at 3615 lb. curb weight, the Daytona had a good potential for competition, and Luigi Chinetti's North American Racing Team (NART) was the first to take advantage of that potential. A stock 365 GTB/4 chassis (No. 12467 GT) was prepared for the 1971 Le Mans 24-hour Grand Prix of Endurance race. Coco Chinetti and Bob Grossman drove the car to 5th overall and thought they had gained 1st in GT class, but the Le Mans organizers awarded 1st in GT to a Porsche 911 driven by the French team of Touroul/Anselme. The excellent showing by Chinetti/Grossman prompted the factory to build a few berlinettas, designating them 365 GTB/4 A *competizione*.

At the time of Ferrari's request for homologation of the 365 GTB/4 in September, 1970, only 390 cars had been produced of the required 500 per year. It was probably suspected that Ferrari was trying to put

Daytona No. 15,685, 6th overall and 2nd in class at Le Mans in 1972 (Posey/Adamowicz) at Riverside Raceway in 1974 for the Road & Track test.

Le Mans test day, 1973 the Andruet/Wollek Daytona almost lifts the inside rear wheel. Right, Road & Track test day, 1970, on Interstate 80, east of Reno, Nevada we see a bit over 7000 in fifth gear and 180 mph which corrects out to 173 mph on a two-way average with a stock 365 GTB/4. Plexiglas-covered lights of the competition Daytona.

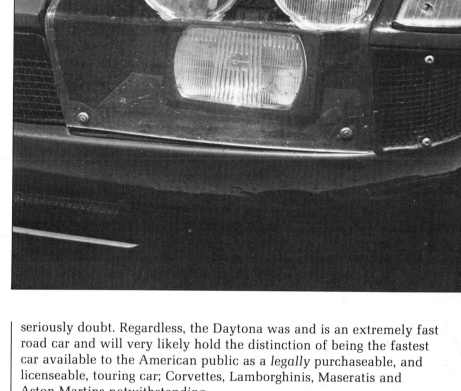

something over on the FIA, but it is significant that this sort of thing seemed to happen more at Le Mans than elsewhere.

Race preparation of the Daytona is much like that of any car being converted from road to track use; lightening wherever possible within the rules (a racing Daytona weighs about 3,200 lbs.—a loss of more than 400 lbs. from stock), wider wheels (15 x 9 front and 15 x 11 rear compared to 15 x 11½ front and rear stock), racing tires (25.0 x 10.0-15 front, 27.0 x 11.0-15 rear), higher compression ratio (10.0:1/9.3:1) and resultant horsepower increase (402 @ 8300 compared to 352 @ 7500).

All this reportedly raised the top speed from 174 to 200 mph, if the engine could achieve the maximum rpm of 8300 in 5th gear—a figure I seriously doubt. Regardless, the Daytona was and is an extremely fast road car and will very likely hold the distinction of being the fastest car available to the American public as a *legally* purchaseable, and licenseable, touring car; Corvettes, Lamborghinis, Maseratis and Aston Martins notwithstanding.

The Daytona chassis is typical Ferrari of the period; tubular (oval) steel frame with full independent suspension, using unequal length A-arms, tubular shocks, coil springs and anti-roll bar at both front and back. The 5-speed, all-synchromesh transmission is in unit with the rear axle and brakes are Dunlop ventilated discs all around. The wheelbase is 2400mm (94.5 inches).

The heart of the car—as with any Ferrari—is the engine. In this case, a 4.4 liter, 4-cam V-12. Carburetion is by six 40 DCN 20 twin-choke Webers, mounted on the inside of the engine vee (some late Ferrari 12s had the carburetors mounted between the camshafts of each bank instead of in the engine vee).

Two Marelli distributors supply the spark to the single plug per cylinder. The early Daytonas had 36mm-diameter exhaust valves, but in 1973 two valve sizes—38 or 42mm-diameter became an option, along with changes in cam design. In this form, the bhp rating was 440, and it was found that the 38mm exhaust valve-engine had a better torque curve than the 42mm design.

Other than this, the factory offered two axle ratios; 3.30:1 and 3.90:1, and that was about all one needed or could get for his Daytona.

The Achilles heel of the GTB/4 Daytona in competition was its brakes. Daytonas ran against Porsche 911s which weighed 1200 lbs. less, and had 12 inch ventilated discs from the 917-30. Cornering ability of the two cars was about the same, but the Porsche was able to maintain its top speed longer because it could go deeper into the turns. Also, the Daytona's brake fluid would boil, further reducing brake effectiveness.

Chinetti added a dual master cylinder (without servo assist) and a better cold air ducting system to the NART Daytonas in 1972. Brake pads still had to be changed after four hours but, by mid-1973, the pads were able to last seven hours in competition.

It appears that four Daytonas were built with aluminum bodies which supposedly lowered the car weight by almost 1000 lbs under the stripped-for-competition steel-bodied Daytona—again, a figure that seems highly unlikely.

A spyder version of the Daytona, the 365 GTS/4, was shown at the Frankfurt show in October 1969, and was produced in limited numbers by Scaglietti on a special order basis. Pininfarina built one Targa-type coupe, which is now in Southern California.

Le Mans, 1972, Jean-Claude Andruet/Claude Ballot-Lena Daytona was 1st in class, 5th overall. Right, Coco Chinetti/Francois Migault 365 GTB/4 was 13th overall at Le Mans in 1973.

Late in 1974, Chinetti's NART took a Daytona to the Bonneville Salt Flats to attack international and national Class C records. The car was similar to a road racing Daytona, but had a front spoiler under the nose, an aluminum radiator, large air inlet tubes for cold air to the carburetors, and brakes from a 512.

Driven by Luigi Chinetti, Jr., Graham Hill and Milt Minter the Daytona achieved national and international Class C records for 10 miles (174.763 mph), 500 kilometers (171.255 mph), 500 miles (166.173 mph) and 1000 kilometers (166.445 mph).

After the 100 kilometer distance a fanbelt broke. It was replaced and then, with Hill at the wheel, the right front tire blew, tangling the front suspension and brake with steel wire from the radial tire.

A rare opportunity presented itself in 1974 when *Road & Track* magazine tested a stock, American-equipped (emissions) Daytona and a racing Daytona at Riverside Raceway.

The stock version was purchased in 1971 by Joe Parkhurst who took delivery in Europe and then shipped it home by boat to Los Angeles harbor. The Competition Daytona was Ken Starbird's NART car driven by Sam Posey and Tony Adamowicz at Le Mans in 1972, finishing 6th overall and 2nd in GT class.

Completing the day, Sam Posey was there to put both cars through their paces. Sam took to the track in the stock Daytona first, and even though he had never driven a production version of the car before, he started with a lap time of 1 minute 48.2 seconds and within five laps had reduced his time to 1 minute, 45.7 seconds. Sam's comment was, "It's fantastic. I've never driven a street car that can do what this one

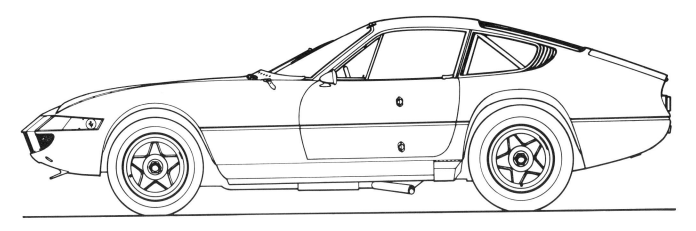

365 GTB/4

1/24 scale drawing based on Ferrari No. 15685

ENGINE

Type ....Lampredi-based, water-cooled, 60 degree V-12
Bore/stroke, mm/inches 81.0/71.0, 3.205/2.81
Displacement, cc/cubic inches...............................4390/267.8
Valve operation: Double overhead camshafts on each bank with cup and spacers operating directly on inclined valves
Valve springs ....Coil
Camshaft drive...Chain
Ignition ....Two Marelli distributors
Sparkplugs/cyl ....One
Compression ratio 10.1:1
Carburetion ....Six Weber 40 DCN twin-choke, downdraft
BHP (Mfg.) ....402 @ 8300 rpm

DRIVE TRAIN

Clutch ....Single dry-plate
Transmission: Five-speed, all synchromesh, in unit with differential
Rear axle ....Transaxle with halfshafts
Axle ratios 3.30, 3.50:1

CHASSIS

Frame ....Welded tubular steel
Wheelbase, mm/inches 2400/94.5
Track, front, mm/inches 1490/58.7
    rear, mm/inches...1475/58.1
Front suspension: Independent, unequal-length A-arms, coil springs
Rear suspension: Independent, unequal-length A-arms, coil springs
Shock absorbers..Tubular
Brakes ....Disc
Tire size, front/rear............................10.0–25.0/11.0–27.0 x 15
Wheels ....Campagnolo alloy, center-lock, hex nut

GENERAL

Length overall, mm/inches 4395/169.1
Width 1840/72.4
Height...1220/48.0
Body builder ....Scaglietti (Pininfarina design)

can—handling, power, predictability, it has it all."

The only faults Sam found were too-soft springs and shocks, making it necessary to apply throttle carefully when exiting a turn. And in a high-speed curve, such as Riverside's turn nine, the understeer usually associated with front-engined cars wasn't there.

Climbing into the competition Daytona, Sam turned a first lap of 1 minute 39.7 seconds and finally a 1:37.0, without straining himself or the car.

The power difference (352 @ 7500/402 @ 8300) wasn't particularly noticeable to Sam but cornering ability was. This was due in part to tires as proved the day before on a skidpad when the stock Daytona recorded 0.817g with its Michelin XVR tires, and the competition Daytona achieved 0.952g with its ultra-wide Goodyear Blue Streaks.

Before the day was over, Posey had reduced his lap times to 1:35.2 in the racing model and 1:44.0 in the stocker, a difference of 8.8 seconds on a 2.5 mile track. As a comparison, the same day Sam drove Steve Earle's 1963 250 GTO around Riverside in 1:40.4 after only three laps.

There is a mixed reaction to the Daytona's styling; one group calling it dated and cliche-ridden, the other calling it the best-ever Ferrari. But both sides agree on driving and performance. It is, simply, fantastic.

The Daytona will idle along in bumper-to-bumper traffic, without any apparent ill effects yet, when open country is reached, it will out-perform almost anything on the road with disconcerting ease.

I took part in the R&T test of the Daytona in 1970 and must confess to some trepidation about the flat-out high speed run we wanted to make. The front end design looked to me like we would get some lifting and possible loss of control, and during our acceleration tests it seemed to be true. But when we took the car out early the following morning for the high speed run it ran straight and true without a bit of float, wandering, or loss of steering right up to an indicated 180 mph.

Competition Daytona has flared fenders to cover wider tires, special latches to secure rear deck lid and metal straps to prevent rear window from lifting out at speed.

And any enthusiast, whether he likes Ferraris or not, *has* to be impressed with a shift from fourth to fifth gear at 140 mph. Most cars are completely out of steam at that speed, and we were still accelerating at a rate that was very pronounced; a rate that was maintained until we reached about 170 on the speedometer.

I've driven faster, I've driven in more comfort, I've driven cars that were better looking, or more docile, but I've never driven any car with the combination of Grand Touring attributes wrapped up in one machine that can compare to the Daytona.

365 GT4/BB

After starting with a 1.5 liter V-12 engine in 1947, Ferrari had built two, four and six cylinder inline engines and vee types in V-6 and V-8 configurations.

In 1964, the first flat, opposed engine was built at Ferrari; a 12-cylinder, 1.5 liter Formula 1 with Lucas injection. It had 11.0:1 compression ratio and developed 210 bhp at 11,000 rpm (compared to 72 bhp at 5600 of that first Ferrari 1.5 liter 12, 17 years earlier).

The flat "boxer" engine debuted at the 1964 Italian Grand Prix at Monza, but didn't actually race until the U.S. Grand Prix at Watkins Glen in October. John Surtees, Lorenzo Bandini and Pedro Rodriguez drove Ferraris with the horizontally opposed twelve during the 1965 season and while it proved reliable, it didn't win a Grand Prix.

A similar engine, in 2-liter form, appeared at the end of 1967 in a Dino 206 S chassis. The car was called the Sport 2000 and was built to compete in the 1968 European Mountain Championship. It didn't run in 1968, and the engine reappeared in a more developed Dino chassis in 1969 as the 212 E *Montagna*.

A 3-liter "Boxer", the 312 B Formula 1 car, came out in 1970 and was followed by a prototype sports/racing version—the 312 PB. The flat 12 engine proved extremely successful in racing, in both Grand Prix and Sports Prototype events, and it would seem natural that the layout would be used for a road car.

The Pininfarina-designed Berlinetta Boxer, a 2-seat GT car, made its debut at the 1971 Turin Auto Show, and went into limited production in 1973 as the 365 GT4/BB. The engine was a 4-cam, 4.4 liter flat 12 located behind the driver, but ahead of the rear axle.

The main body structure was steel, but the front hood, doors and rear deck lid (actually the engine compartment cover) were aluminum

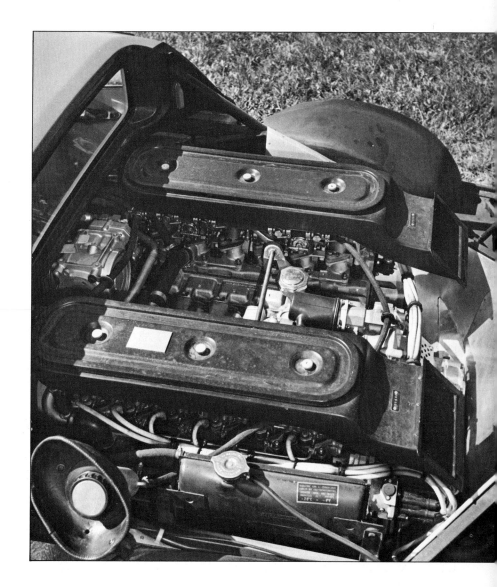

and the lower body sections were fiberglass. Visually, the 365 GT4/BB resembled the Dino, but had a taut, purposeful look that simply said "power." There was more overhang at the front than at the back, and the wheels looked almost too large for the relatively small package.

The retractable headlights were at the outboard edges of the hood/fender area, and back from the low front edge far enough to give them barely minimum legal height when open.

The radiator was in the nose with an air intake in the matte black area below the body break line. The familiar Ferrari egg crate grille and prancing horse were there, but not as prominently displayed as on previous Ferraris.

All Boxers, no matter what the top body color has been, have had the lower body in matte black, with black windshield and window trim. Bodies are assembled in Modena by Scaglietti.

The wheelbase was fairly long at 2500mm (98.4 inches) which is almost four inches longer than the Daytona (94.5 inches) and was necessary because of the long 12 cylinder engine behind the driver. This was the first Ferrari to have this wheelbase since the 330 LMB most being shorter, at 2400mm (94.5 inches), or longer, at 2600mm (102.3 inches).

Overall length of the Boxer was 171.7 inches, width 70.9, and height 44.0 inches, track was 59.1 inches front and 59.8 rear. Disc brakes and 5-speed transmissions were used—as on all current Ferraris—but in this case the transmission and differential were in unit in a rear transaxle.

Suspension was independent all around, by unequal-length A-arms, coil springs, tubular shocks and anti-roll bars at front and rear. Between the prototype and production, round and oval tubing chassis members gave way for easier-to-fabricate square and rectangular tubing.

The flat 12 engine had toothed-belt-driven double overhead camshafts on each bank, with intake ports and cams on the top, exhaust ports and cams on the lower side. Four 3-throat Weber 40

IF3C carburetors fed through 12 ports with a single intake valve for each cylinder.

Compression ratio was 8.8:1, cylinder bore was 81mm, stroke 71mm, for a displacement of 4390cc and 380 horsepower was

Leather-covered wheel and instruments recessed into panel characterize "Boxer" interior, and right, Claude Ballot-Lena in the race-prepared NART GT4/BB.

One articulated windshield wiper serves large windshield area, and air conditioning vents are placed at top of instrument panel. NART competition modifications include carburetor air boxes, extra fuel tank in right side of cockpit, superwide tires with rebuilt fenders to cover.

produced at 7200 rpm. Top speed for the BB was claimed to be 187 mph, which seemed reasonable considering frontal area, body shape and available power, but a *Road & Track* road test (June 1975 issue) resulted in "only" 175 mph.

In spite of the flat layout's resemblance to the 312 series, the BB engine owes more to the 60-degree, 4.4 liter V-12 used in the 365 GTC/4. Bore, stroke and displacement are identical and rods, pistons and valve gear are interchangeable between the two engines.

The 5-speed transmission, controlled by a gated lever, has all indirect gears and, with a final drive ratio of 3.75:1, the top ratio is 3.08:1. The shift mechanism is excellent for a mid-engined car although some problems have occured in full throttle, high rpm shifting which was probably due to either flexing of the linkage or engine movement under load.

The clutch is stiff, the gated shift lever takes some practice before one becomes familiar with it, and with a high first gear, fast smooth starts are difficult for the driver who isn't accustomed to the Boxer. And, with a curb weight of 3420 pounds, acceleration isn't

breathtaking but can be described as a great deal more than adequate—particularly once the car has reached about 40 mph in first gear.

Handling is a delight for an enthusiastic, capable driver. The steering, heavy at low speeds, lightens up as speed increases and has considerable road feel. The combination of tail-heavy weight distribution (43/57) and understeer designed into the chassis results in an agile, maneuverable car.

There is little doubt that Ferraris will continue to be built for many years to come as the current management under Enzo Ferrari is sympathetic to the Ferrari mystique. And Fiat, as 50 percent owner of Ferrari stock, realizes the value of keeping the name alive.

But, due to the ever-increasing fuel costs driving speed limits down, and over zealous safety minded bureaucrats imposing ever tougher legislation for the design and construction of automobiles, it is doubtful that any road-going, customer Ferrari of the future will ever have the performance, pizazz or sheer animal magnetism of the 365 GT4/BB.

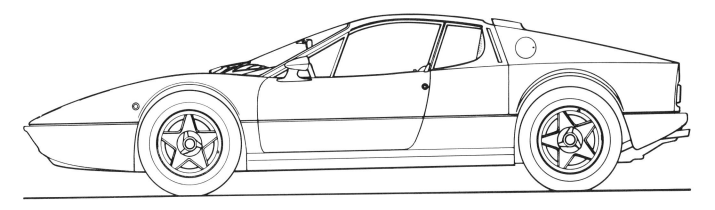

365 GT4/BB

1/24 scale drawing based on Ferrari No. 17553

ENGINE

Type ....Forghieri-designed, water-cooled 180 degree flat-12
Bore/stroke, mm/inches 81.0/71.0, 3.205/2.81
Displacement, cc/cubic inches 4390/267.8
Valve operation: Double overhead camshafts on each bank with
   cups and spacers operating directly on inclined valves
Valve springs ....Coil
Camshaft drive ....Toothed belt
Ignition ....Dinoplex transister
Sparkplugs/cyl ....One
Compression ratio 8.8:1
Carburetion ....Four Weber 40 IF3C three-choke, downdraft
BHP (Mfg.) ....380 @ 7200 rpm

DRIVE TRAIN

Clutch ....Single dry-plate
Transmission: Five-speed, all synchromesh, direct drive in 5th
   gear
Rear axle ....Transaxle below crankshaft, with halfshafts
Axle ratios 3.50:1

CHASSIS

Frame ....Tubular steel with aluminum skin
Wheelbase, mm/inches 2500/98.4
Track, front, mm/inches 1500/59.1
   rear, mm/inches..1520/59.8
Front suspension: Independent, unequal-length A-arms, coil
   springs
Rear suspension: Independent, unequal-length A-arms, coil
   springs
Shock absorbers..Tubular
Brakes ....Disc
Tire size, front/rear..215 x 15
Wheels....................Campagnolo alloy, center-lock, knock-off

GENERAL

Length overall, mm/inches 4360/171.7
Width 1800/70.9
Height..1120/44.1
Body builder ....Scaglietti (Pininfarina design)

512 BB

In late 1976 a 512 BB was announced as a replacement for the 365 GT4/BB. At first glance the two models look identical. Then one notices the "chin" spoiler, or air dam, under the front grille, and the NASA ducts on the lower body sides just in front of the rear wheels of the 512. These ducts are to direct cool air to the exhaust headers.

In spite of an extra 552cc (4942 compared to 4390), the 512 is rated at "only" 360 bhp compared to the 380 bhp for the 365. It would also seem that Ferrari has returned to the style of designation used on the Dinos (512: 5 liters, 12 cylinders) rather than his off and on again "normal" style (365: 365cc per cylinder x 12 = 4390cc displacement).

Other major specifications, design, and layout are as before. Factory claimed speeds are 58 in 1st, 81 in 2nd, 107 in 3rd, 141 in 4th and 188 top, with 0–400 meters in 13.7 seconds. Zero to one kilometer (⅝ mile) takes 24 seconds with a terminal speed of 154 mph at the kilometer.

ENGINE	250 GTO	250 GTO 64	250 LM	330 LMB	330 P2/3	330 P3
Designer	Colombo[1]	Colombo[1]	Colombo[1]	Lampredi[2]	Lampredi[2]	Lampredi[2]
Type	V-12	V-12	V-12	V-12	V-12	V-12
Bore x Stroke, mm	73.0 x 58.8	73.0 x 58.8	77.0 x 58.8	77.0 x 71.0	77.0 x 71.0	77.0 x 71.0
Bore x Stroke, in	2.875 x 2.315	2.875 x 2.315	3.05 x 2.314	3.05 x 2.81	3.05 x 2.81	3.05 x 2.81
Displacement, cc/in	2953/180.0	2953/180.0	3286/200.5	3967/242.0	3967/242.0	3967/242.0
Compression Ratio	9.8:1	9.8:1	9.8:1	9.0:1	10.5:1	10.5:1
Camshaft Layout	S.O./Bank	S.O./Bank	S.O./Bank	S.O./Bank	D.O.H.C.	D.O.H.C.
Camshaft Drive	Chain	Chain	Chain	Chain	Chain	Chain
Cam Followers	Roller	Roller	Roller	Roller	Cup	Cup
Valves—Design, Number	Inc, 2/cyl	Inc, 2/cyl	Inc, 2/Cyl	Inc, 2/Cyl	Inc, 2/Cyl	Inc, 2/Cyl
Valve Springs	Coil	Coil	Coil	Coil	Coil	Coil
Sparkplugs/Cylinder	1	1	1	1	2	2
Ignition	2 Distributors	2 Distributors	2 Distributors	2 Distributors	2 Distributors	2 Distributors
Carburetors—No, Type	6-38 DCN	6-38 DCN	6-38 DCN	6-42 DCN	Lucas Injection	Lucas Injection
BHP/RPM	295/7400	300/7700	305/7500	400/7500	420/8200	420/8200
Location	Front	Front	Rear	Front	Rear	Rear

DRIVE TRAIN						
Clutch	Single Dry-Plate	Single Dry-Plate	Single Dry-Plate[5]	Single Dry-Plate	Single Dry-Plate	Single Dry-Plate
Transmission—Gears	5-Speed & Rev	5-Speed & Rev	5-Speed & Rev	4-Speed & Rev	5-Speed & Rev	5-Speed & Rev
Type	2-5 Synchro	2-5 Synchro	Non-Synchro	All-Synchro	ZF All-Synchro	ZF All-Synchro
Location	With Engine	With Engine	Rear Transaxle	With Engine	Rear Transaxle	Rear Transaxle
Axle ratios	3.67, 3.78, 4.00, 4.25, 4.55, 4.57, 4.86:1	3.67, 3.78, 4.00, 4.25 4.55, 4.57, 4.86:1	3.548, 4.038, 4.426, 4.842:1	3.67, 3.72, 4.00, 4.25, 4.55, 4.57, 4.86:1		

(1) Based on Colombo design, developed by Massimino and Chiti
(2) Lampredi design developed by Ferrari engineering staff

(3) Based on Colombo design, developed by Rocchi and Forghieri
(4) Based on 312 B layout, developed with 365 components by Ferrari staff
(5) Some cars had multi-disc clutch

330 P4	312 P	512 S	512 M	275 GTB Comp	365 GTB/4	365 GTB/4 Comp	365 GT/BB
Rocchi	Forghieri/Rocchi	Marelli/Rocchi	Marelli/Rocchi	Colombo [3]	Lampredi[2]	Lampredi[2]	Forghieri[4]
V-12	V-12	V-12	V-12	V-12	V-12	V-12	Flat-12
77.0 x 71.0	77.0 x 53.5	87.0 x 70.0	87.0 x 70.0	77.0 x 58.8	81.0 x 71.0	81.0 x 71.0	81.0 x 71.0
3.05 x 2.81	3.05 x 2.12	3.48 x 2.77	3.48 x 2.77	3.05 x 2.315	3.205 x 2.81	3.205 x 2.81	3.205 x 2.81
3967/242.0	2990/182.4	4994/274.1	4994/274.1	3286/200.5	4390/267.8	4390/267.8	4390/267.8
11.0:1	11.0:1	11.8:1	11.8:1	9.7:1	9.3:1	10.1:1	8.8:1
D.O.H.C.	D.O.H.C.	D.O.H.C.	D.O.H.C.	S.O./Bank	D.O.H.C.	D.O.H.C.	D.O.H.C.
Chain	Chain	Chain	Chain	Chain	Chain	Chain	Toothed Belt
Cup	Cup	Cup	Cup	Roller	Cup	Cup	Cup
Inc, 3/Cyl	Inc, 3/Cyl	Inc, 2/Cyl	Inc, 2/Cyl	Inc, 2/Cyl	inc, 2/Cyl	Inc, 2/Cyl	Inc, 2/Cyl
Coil	Coil	Coil	Coil	Coil	Coil	Coil	Coil
2	1	1	1	1	1	1	1
2 Distributors	2 Distributors	Dinoplex Transistor	Dinoplex Transistor	2 Distributors	2 Distributors	2 Distributors	Dinoplex Transistor
Lucas Injection	Lucas Injection	Lucas Injection	Lucas Injection	6-40 DCZ6	6-40 DCN	6-40 DCN	4-40 IF3C
450/8000	430/9800	550/8500	610/9000	320/7700	352/7500	402/8300	380/7200
Rear	Rear	Rear	Rear	Front	Front	Front	Rear
Single Dry-Plate	Single Dry-Plate	Multi-Disc	Multi-Disc	Single Dry-Plate	Single Dry-Plate	Single Dry-Plate	Single Dry-Plate
5-Speed & Rev	5-Speed & Rev	5-Speed & Rev	5-Speed & Rev	5-Speed & Rev	5-Speed & Rev	5-Speed & Rev	5-Speed & Rev
ZF All-Synchro	ZF All-Synchro	ZF All Synchro	ZF All-Synchro	ZF All-Synchro	ZF All-Synchro	ZF All-Synchro	All-Synchro
Rear Transaxle	Rear Transaxle	Rear Transaxle	Rear Transaxle	With Rear Axle	With Rear Axle	With Rear Axle	Rear Transaxle[5]
		3.18, 3.40, 3.78, 4.25:1	3.18, 3.40, 3.78, 4.25;1	3.30, 3.50:1	3.30:1	3.30, 3.50;1	3.50:1

(5) Mounted at rear of engine, below crankshaft.

CHASSIS	250 GTO	250 GTO 64	250 LM	330 LMB	275 P2	330 P3
Frame	Welded Tube	Welded Tube	Welded Tube	Welded Tube	Tube & Sheet Skin	Tube & Sheet Skin
Wheelbase—mm/in	2400/94.5	2400/94.5	2400/94.5	2500/98.4	2400/94.5	2400/94.5
Track, Front—mm/in	1354/53.3	1377/54.2	1350/53.1	1422/56.0	1350/53.1	1462/57.6
Track, Rear—mm/in	1350/53.1	1426/56.1	1340/52.8	1414/55.7	1340/52.8	1431/56.3
Suspension—Front	Independent	Independent	Independent	Independent	Independent	Independent
Type	Un. Length A-Arms	Un. Length A-Arms	Un. Length A-Arms	Un. Length A-Arms	Un. Length A-Arms	Un. Length A-Arms
Springs	Coils	Coils	Coils	Coils	Coils	Coils
Suspension—Rear	Rigid Axle	Rigid Axle	Un. length A-Arms	Rigid Axle	Un. Length A-Arms	Un. Upper/Lower Arms
Springs	Semi-Ellip w/Coils	Semi-Ellip w/Coils	Coils	Semi-Ellip w/Coils	Coils	Coils
Shock Absorbers	Tubular	Tubular	Tubular	Tubular	Tubular	Tubular
Brakes	Disc	Disc	Disc	Disc	Disc	Disc
Wheels	Borrani Wire	Borrani Wire	Borrani Wire	Borrani Wire	Borrani Wire[1]	Campagnolo Alloy
Tires—Front/Rear	5.50/7.00 x 15	5.50/7.00 x 15	5.50/7.00 x 15	6.00/7.00 x 15	5.50/7.00 x 15	5.50/7.00 x 15

GENERAL						
Body Designer	Factory	Factory	Factory[2]	Factory [3]	Factory	Factory
Body Builder	Scaglietti	Scaglietti	Scaglietti	Scaglietti	Drogo	Drogo
Length—mm/in	4400/173.2	4210/165.7	4270/168.1	4485/176.6	4260/167.7	4185/164.8
Width—mm/in	1675/65.9	1760/69.3	1700/66.9	1750/68.9	1675/65.9	1810/71.3
Height—mm/in	1245/49.0	1140/44.9	1115/43.9	1275/50.2	1000/39.4	1000/39.4

(1) Campagnolo slotted disc wheels fitted on later cars
(2) Factory design refined for production by Pininfarina

(3) Factory design which was basis for Pininfarina's Berlinetta Lusso
(4) Many detail changes by factory for competition

330 P4	312 P	512 S	512 M	275 GTB Comp	365 GTB/4	365 GTB/4 Comp	365 GT/BB
Tube & Sheet Skin	Tube & Sheet Skin	Tube & Sheet Skin	Tube & Sheet Skin	Welded Tube	Welded Tube	Welded Tube	Tube & Sheet Skin
2400/94.5	2370/93.3	2400/94.5	2400/94.5	2400/94.5	2400/94.5	2400/94.5	2500/98.4
1488/58.6	1485/58.5	1518/59.8	1518/59.8	1377/54.2	1440/56.7	1490/58.7	1500/59.1
1450/57.1	1500/59.1	1511/59.5	1511/59.5	1393/54.8	1425/56.1	1475/58.1	1520/59.8
Independent	Independent	Independent	Independent	Independent	Independent	Independent	Independent
Un. Length A-Arms	Un. Length A-Arms	Un. Length A-Arms	Un. Length A-Arms	Un. Length A-Arms	Un. Length A-Arms	Un. Length A-Arms	Un. Length A-Arms
Coils	Coils	Coils	Coils	Coils	Coils	Coils	Coils
Un. Upper/Lower Arms	Un. Upper/Lower Arms	Un. Upper/Lower Arms	Un. Upper/Lower Arms	Un. Length A-Arms	Un. Length A-Arms	Un. Length A-Arms	Un. Length A-Arms
Coils	Coils	Coils	Coils	Coils	Coils	Coils	Coils
Tubular	Tubular	Tubular	Tubular	Tubular	Tubular	Tubular	Tubular
Disc	Disc	Disc	Disc	Disc	Disc	Disc	Disc
Campagnolo Alloy	Campagnolo Alloy	Campagnolo Alloy	Campagnolo Alloy	Borrani Wire	Campagnolo Alloy	Campagnolo Alloy	Campagnolo Alloy
4.75-10.30/ 6.00-12.30 x 15	4.75-10.30/ 6.00-13.50 x 15	4.25-11.50/ 6.00-14.50 x 15	4.25-11.50/ 6.00-14.50 x 15	5.50/7.00 x 15	200 x 15	10.0-25.0/ 11.0-27.0 x 15	215 x 15
Factory	Factory	Factory	Factory	Pininfarina(4)	Pininfarina	Pininfarina	Pininfarina
Drogo	Drogo	Drogo	Drogo	Scaglietti	Scaglietti	Scaglietti	Scaglietti
4185/164.8	4230/166.5	4060/159.8(5)	4360/171.7	4280/168.5	4425/174.2	4395/169.1	4360/171.7
1810/71.3	1980/77.9	2000/78.7	2000/78.7	1685/66.3	1760/69.3	1840/72.4	1800/70.9
1000/39.4	950/37.4(6)	970/38.2	970/38.2	1350/53.1	1245/49.0	1220/48.0	1120/44.1

(5) Original car, later examples approx. 4250/167.3; Le Mans long-tail approx. 4500/177.2
(6) Estimated for Berlinetta; height of Spyder 890/35.0 at rollbar.

BOOK DESIGN by Chuck Queener

ACKNOWLEDGEMENTS

All books are the result of the combined efforts of many persons. Even though I am both author and publisher, this book could not have been published without the expert help of the following:
COVER COLOR SEPARATION—Roberts Graphic Arts,
  El Monte, Calif.
TYPESETTING—Computer Typesetting Services, Glendale, Calif.
RESEARCH INFORMATION (Publications) *Ferrari The Sports & GT Cars* by Fitzgerald & Merritt revised by Jonathan Thompson, *Ferrari* by Hans Tanner, *Road & Track, Sports Car Illustrated/Car and Driver, Autocourse, Automobile Year, Ferrari*—publication of the Ferrari Owners Club. (Individuals) Steve Earle, Steve Griswold, Bill Lester, Fred Leydorf, Bill Rudd, Chuck Queener, and particular thanks to Ed Niles and Jess Pourret.

And special thanks to those who let us photograph their cars
250 GTO Steve Earle
250 LM Kerry Payne
275 GTB/C Ed Niles
365 GTB/4 Ken Starbird
365 GT4/BB Bill Harrah/Modern Classic Motors

PHOTO CREDITS

Dean Batchelor, Pete Coltrin, Ferrari, Geoff Goddard, Phil Hill, John Lamm, Henry Manney, Kurt Miska, Gunther Molter, Pininfarina, Chuck Queener, Jerry Sloniger, Bill Warner.

Scale Drawings by Jonathan Thompson

BOOKS IN THE CLASSIC SPORTS CAR SERIES
from Dean Batchelor Publications
FERRARI The Early Berlinettas & Competition Coupes—
  October, 1974
FERRARI The Early Spyders & Competition Roadsters—April, 1975
FERRARI The Gran Turismo & Competition Berlinettas—Dec., 1977
PORSCHE The 4-Cylinder, 4-Cam Sports & Racing Cars—Dec., 1977
and soon to be published:
FERRARI The Sports & Sports Prototype Competition Cars